# Stay the Course

## GOD'S BLUEPRINT FOR YOUR DESTINY IN THIS PRESENT MOVE OF GOD

Camilla Charles

CAMILLA CHARLES

Scriptures marked AMP are taken from the AMPLIFIED BIBLE (AMP): Scripture taken from the AMPLIFIED® BIBLE, Copyright © 1954, 1958, 1962, 1964, 1965, 1987 by the Lockman Foundation. Used by Permission. All rights reserved.

Scriptures marked NKJV are taken from the NEW KING JAMES VERSION (NKJV): Scripture taken from the NEW KING JAMES VERSION®. Copyright© 1982 by Thomas Nelson, Inc. Used by permission. All rights reserved.

Scriptures marked HCSB are taken from the HOLMAN CHRISTIAN STANDARD BIBLE (HCSB): Scripture taken from the HOLMAN CHRISTIAN STANDARD BIBLE, copyright© 1999, 2000, 2002, 2003 by Holman Bible Publishers, Nashville Tennessee. All rights reserved.

Scriptures marked NLT are taken from the HOLY BIBLE, NEW LIVING TRANSLATION (NLT): Scriptures taken from the HOLY BIBLE, NEW LIVING TRANSLATION, Copyright© 1996, 2004, 2007, 2013 by Tyndale House Foundation. Used by permission of Tyndale House Publishers, Inc., Carol Stream, Illinois 60188. All rights reserved.

Scripture quotations marked Passion Translation, TPT, are taken from Song of Songs, Divine Romance, The Passion Translation, Copyright 2014. Used by permission of BroadStreet Publishing Group, LLC, Racine, Wisconsin, USA. All rights reserved.

Scripture quotations marked MSG, THE MESSAGE are taken from THE MESSAGE, Copyright © by Eugene H. Peterson 1993, 1994, 1995, 1996, 2000, 2001, 2002. Used by permission of NavPress. All rights reserved. Represented by Tyndale House Publishers, Inc.

Copyright © 2017 Camilla Charles

All rights reserved.

ISBN: 1-946106-08-9
ISBN-13: 978-1-946106-08-7


Glorified Publishing
PO Box 8004
The Woodlands, TX 77387
www.GlorifiedPublishing.com

# CONTENTS

| | | |
|---|---|---|
| | Endorsements | v |
| | Acknowledgments | ix |
| | Introduction | 1 |
| 1 | Come Up Here | 9 |
| 2 | Winds of Change | 21 |
| 3 | New Wine Skins | 35 |
| 4 | Baptism of Love | 51 |
| 5 | Let's Cross Over | 65 |
| 6 | Generous Living | 77 |
| 7 | Wide Open Spaces | 91 |
| 8 | Yellow Walls, Butterflies and Fives | 103 |
| 9 | Grace to Stay | 113 |
| 10 | From Declaration to Demonstration | 129 |
| 11 | Experience His Presence, See His Glory | 141 |

CAMILLA CHARLES

# Endorsements

I love the passion that Camilla Charles has for the Kingdom of God. When I first met her, I knew she was a woman who loved the Lord and was committed to a life journey with Him. She has helped many walk with the Lord. Through her book, she can help you.

Patricia King
Patricia King Ministries  patriciaking.com

*Camilla Charles new book- Stay the Course, will help and guide you to walk out God's specially designed blueprint for your life and destiny. Camilla is an amazing author, speaker and one of the most genuine people that I have met. I encourage you to pick up this book, and get ready to run the race with faith, hope and love. You will not be disappointed.*

*John Perks*
*Breakthrough Ministries International,*
*Eyes and Wings/ Be A Hero  Canada* breakthroughministries.ca


Camilla Charles is my friend and a beacon of hope in this generation. She is a living breathing example of what her wonderful book "Stay The Course" shines a revelatory light on. In the face of dark circumstances and pain, God is good and He has good plans for each of us, to give us hope and a future! Drink in these encouraging words from a battle tested warrior who has paid the price for her revival.

Keith Luker, Revivalist
Outpouring Ministries
Redding, California

*Thank you very much, Camilla, for addressing and touching this so important topic. You are a person who sensitively responds to the Holy Spirit, and I am quite sure that many will benefit from this book - people as well as cities and nations. For God has called people and nations - take Israel for example. This book comes out at the right time. I pray that it will be a blessing to many. Altogether an exciting topic in our days.*

*Walter Heidenreich, International Evangelist*
*President of FCJG and HELP International*
*Lüdenscheid, Germany*

Camilla Charles is a revivalist in the truest sense of the word. Her tenacity to see her city, her region, and her nation from God's eternal perspective and then to follow through with this heavenly vision by her words and actions will inspire you. Her book will encourage you and provoke you to action. Camilla has truly captured God's Spirit in Stay the Course. We WILL see the glory of God in the land of the living. For those who desire to align with all God has planned for our beautiful nation, this book will add fuel to your revival fire.

Judy Capps
President of Hope Ministries of Northeast Texas
Co-owner of The Landing Event Center, Mt Pleasant, Texas

*In a time when revival is a must, a voice can be heard crying out from East Texas. That voice belongs to Camilla Charles. Camilla is relentless in shining light on the path to revival. Her Jesus inspired words will leap off the page into your spirit and ignite a fire that cannot be quenched. I am a lifetime friend of Camilla and I believe her revolutionary book will become your war cry, your go to when you need your spirit steadied. If you've ever wondered if it's possible to receive an anointing to contend for revival by reading a book, "Stay the Course" will answer that question for you with a strong affirmative. Read it. Envision it. Experience it. "Stay the Course."*

*Enoch Rich, Pastor*
*Living Word Church*
*Central City, Kentucky*

I am very excited about the release of "Stay the Course" and believe the message of this book is crucial for our time and generation. Camilla lives and embodies what she writes about. I know her as a woman who relentlessly pursues the presence of God. She is determined to follow and obey the Holy Spirit every step of the way – and loves Jesus with her whole heart. Camilla is a huge example to me personally and a great inspiration through her lifestyle of worship, humility and persistence. This book will not only encourage and challenge, but also enable and equip you to run the race set before you.

Merisha Janke
Help for all Nations
Austin, Texas

*I am happy to introduce you to a wealth of encouragement and direction. In a time when life is fluid and in constant flux it is important to stay the course. Camilla Charles has captured the essence of Jesus instructing us to not be easily moved away from truth. Aren't you thankful, Jesus stayed his course? He had the right to cast off His destiny when circumstances were adverse but instead He prayed, "not my will but yours be done." The book you hold in your hand you will want to read over and over to remind yourself to stay the course and not come short of His Glory. Thank you Camilla for helping us to stay focused on what lies ahead of us and how to get to our destiny.*

*Kerry Kirkwood*
*Pastor, Author*
*Trinity Fellowship Church*
*Tyler Texas*


"Stay the Course" has an amazing message for the Church as we finalize the message of Jesus before the trumpet sounds. The culture of revival will become normal for the Church. If you can hear Jesus calling your name through the pages of this book - then be encouraged to "Stay the Course."

Lynn McKenzie
Road 2 Glory Ministry
Women's Professional Rodeo Association World Champion Barrel Racer 1978, 1981.
Lindale, Texas

## ACKNOWLEDGMENTS

Steven-my best friend and partner for life. Thank you for making me laugh and for all of those convertible rides into the wide open spaces. This is the Lord's doing and it is marvelous in our eyes. Thank you for pushing me forward into my destiny. I will forever love you.

Cameron and Christian-you are my treasure and the best thing that ever happened to your dad and I. I am beyond proud of the young men you have become. I look forward to the pages of life that God is writing on you and through you. All my love to you.

My family, friends and Bethesda family-thank you for being my constant joy. I love you and I thank you for your love and support.

My Stay the Course team-Wendy, Jeremiah, Karen and Edie. Thank you for all you have done and given to make this book a reality.

CAMILLA CHARLES

# Introduction

**"What a gift life is to those who stay the course! You've heard, of course, of Job's staying power, and you know how God brought it all together for him at the end. That's because God cares, cares right down to the last detail." - James 5:11 MSG**

God has designed a special purpose for all of us. He has given us dreams, visions and a destiny for our life. Sometimes, it might just be easier to ignore and move on past that dream or "word from the Lord." We may prefer to retreat, fall back and not push the limits for anything outside of the norm of our comfort zone. We often blame others, outside circumstances, or even God Himself when our destiny is not so easily attained.

But wait...for the dreamers, the persistent ones, the stubborn ones who won't take 'No' for an answer, the childlike who believe beyond what they can accomplish in a God who shines best in the impossible…this book is for you.

This book is for the local church, pastors, intercessors, missionaries and body of Christ that believe for revival and transformation of cities, regions, states and nations … even when the reality is sometimes division, disunity, apathy, unbelief, lack of hope or faith in the midst of shrinking congregations, lack of power, lack of miracles and financial upheaval.

This is for the business men and women who believe in and pray for, a business that will not only affect their community for the better but will finance nations coming to Christ, even when all they see are failed businesses, bad investments and piles of debt.

This is for the mom praying for her children to turn around and come to the Lord, no matter where they are, no matter how deep into the world's system they may have fallen.

This is for you, the ones who still believe, even when it hurts, even when it causes you to look foolish to others and sometimes alienate yourself from friends and family, business partners and church members who believe that you should just move on.

This is for the one who can't move on past the dream, the hope, the vision, the Word of the Lord, the *Rhema* word that's been written in your Bible and hundreds of times in journals, on random pieces of paper, in computer files and documents and in the "notes" section of your smart phone. This is for the ones who won't give up, can't give up, even when everything in you wants to give up. The Spirit of God will anoint (furnish, qualify, empower, cover, enable) you for the task of believing, praying, and not giving up – to Stay the Course until you see it accomplished!

## Stay to See Your Destiny and the Destiny of a City, Region and Nation Accomplished!

In 1885, the phrase "stay the course" originally meant horses holding out till the end of the race. We are in the race of a lifetime!

> "Don't you realize that in a race everyone runs, but only one person gets the prize? So run to win!" - 1 Corinthians 9:24 NLT

According to the Bible, we win!

> "All athletes are disciplined in their training. They do it to win a prize that will fade away, but we do it for an eternal prize."
> - 1 Corinthians 9:25 NLT

Jesus is our victor, our champion and our Captain of the Hosts. He set the standard and paid the ultimate price for our freedom and destiny!

> **"I looked up and saw a white horse standing there. Its rider carried a bow, and a crown was placed on his head. He rode out to win many battles and gain the victory."**
> **- Revelation 6:2 NLT**

We are in a race to see culture changed and nations saved for the glory of God.

> **Culture: the attitudes, customs, and beliefs that distinguish one group of people from another (www.dictionary.com).**

Culture is PEOPLE's attitudes, PEOPLE's customs, and PEOPLE's beliefs. Culture is just a reflection of what's in people's hearts. The only way to change a culture is to change hearts. I believe that God has called people like you and me that will do whatever it takes to see real change in our families, churches, cities, regions, the United States of America and in the nations of the world. We can have that staying power to see an awakening that will bring transformation which ultimately will lead to reformation.

My husband, Steven, and I have been taking ministry teams to Washington, D.C. at least once a year for many years now. We have loved on our capitol and sowed into this nation through prayer, time, investment and community. We love D.C. and our nation and we know that God is moving, even in the midst of political upheaval. We should all know, however, that real change will come as the church awakens and takes its place in society.

In March of 2016, I had the privilege to be a part of a prayer meeting at the U.S. Capitol Building with a team of intercessors. We were hosted by a senator and we prayed in the Senate chamber, the House of Representatives, the Rotunda, Statuary Hall and the old Supreme Court chamber (yes, prayer gatherings like this are happening weekly in D.C.)!

The senator hosting this great prayer meeting said to us, "You are here praying for us. As much as we appreciate and receive what you are doing, we are here praying for you, the church, to rise up and to do what only you can do." Only then will this nation truly turn around. God is releasing strategy and vision to many of us for just that. He is also releasing *the staying anointing*: the grace to stay the course and the strength to see this victory through.

## Preparing YOU for the Multicolored/Multifaceted Present Move of God!

You might ask, "Are we in a present move of God?" The answer is yes! We have been preparing for the next move of God, but have moved from **next** to **present.** The shift has taken place. This is so exciting for every believer in Christ! We have an opportunity to seize the day!

There have been strategic timelines regarding our Bible history, present history, and events that have caused this shift to take place. "Azusa Now 2016" was a huge transition, another shift in the spirit! Many other intercessory prayer and worship gatherings taking place in the Body of Christ in the last few years have caused other spiritual shifts.

This might be the first time you are reading about or hearing that we are in a present move of God. Maybe you don't see it where you live. Maybe you hear about it but it's always another place in the world other than where you live. Maybe you have never even heard of a present-day revival or outpouring taking place. The good news is that God is equipping us to run this race and stay the course for victory. God is preparing us and teaching us what His ways look like.

Multicolored means "having many colors".
Multifaceted means "having many facets".

A facet is, "one side of something many-sided, especially of a cut gem; a particular aspect or feature of something; "participation by the laity in all facets of church life."

Wow! This sounds exciting, and just like our Father, to cause us to be a part of something that will demonstrate who we are as a people, living in HIS GLORY. You and I are as unique and individual as God has made us. This wonderful, present move of God will be demonstrated in many beautiful ways of which we can be a part.

My prayer for you as you read the pages of this book is that you will lock eyes with Jesus, the lover of your soul, in a fresh new way. Also, I pray that you will be encouraged by my story of not giving up, relish what you receive and learn along the way, and be encouraged that as you stay the course and don't give up, you will win!

**"I am not waiting for a move of God, I am a Move of God." – William Booth, founder of the Salvation Army.**

# CAMILLA CHARLES

# Chapter 1

# Come Up Here

> "Then as I looked, I saw a door standing open in heaven, and the same voice I had heard before spoke to me like a trumpet blast. The voice said, "Come up here, and I will show you what must happen after this." And instantly I was in the Spirit, and I saw a throne in heaven and someone sitting on it." - Revelation 4:1-2 NLT

My journey in life will always begin and end with my relationship with the Father, Jesus, and Holy Spirit. It is a beautiful Trinity designed for us, here on earth, and into eternity. I will begin and end this book with relationship and intimacy with Jesus. There is nothing greater! In my opinion, everything we do in life centers on this incredible relationship.

It is amazing that we can have an intimate relationship with the

King of the universe! Jesus gave us the Holy Spirit to have a relationship and commune with on earth. We cannot stay the course if we do not know our course. God designed for us to have a blueprint for our lives. That blueprint can only be found through relationship and intimacy.

A highlight in my life that began this journey of learning to stay the course was when our church was in a season of revival and renewal. At the time, we were serving in my parents' church leading worship and serving as associate pastors there. We had been traveling on the road in ministry but felt the Lord leading us back there full-time to join in what God was doing. As with many in our region and maybe other areas, the revival was not sustained and did not happen in the fullness we felt it should have. We can now say that there were so many life lessons learned in that season that will help us in this present move of God. Like many others in the late 1990's, our lives were forever changed, ruined for the ordinary, and left always want-ing more of God's Presence!

> *"We cannot stay the course if we do not know our course. God designed for us to have a blueprint for our life. That blueprint can only be found through relationship and intimacy."*

During that season of revival, life stood still for a time. Everything was alive and exciting! I have always had a wonderful relationship with Jesus and I am so grateful for my spiritual heritage, but during this season revival was birthed in me and a fire was lit that has never, and I pray will never, go out. However, it was during that season when our plans failed, or so it seemed, that I knew I would always be a part of revival, part of awakening and have a desire for transformation.

What we thought would be revival meetings for life, or at least for a very long time, through a series of events came to an end. It seemed that life was fragile and hopeless, producing much hope deferred in our life. This sounds dramatic and somewhat comical now because we have learned that we can live in a revival culture and that we carry revival and awakening everywhere we go. I will say, though, that God has set times that He chooses to meet with people for seasons of reviving, renewal and awakening that happen corporately, and many times during a series of meetings. Momentum is gained during this time and God releases a deposit of His Glory that cannot happen any other way.

> *"Through intimacy with Him comes knowledge of who we are in Christ – our identity. This, in turn, enables us to walk in the God-given authority that we carry as believers."*

I feel very privileged to have grown up during the tent revivals still going on in the late 1960's, where night after night, for weeks and months at a time, the Glory came and lives were changed. Although I was very young then, that influence has impacted me for my entire life.

During the season of transition in the late 1990's and into 2000, the Lord began to teach me and put into me the desire to have a staying anointing. He put in me the desire to not give up on the call on my life for revival, awakening, and transformation of lives and nations just because I felt that it was taken, stolen or dead. He put in me a pioneering spirit! He gave me the forerunner spirit! He put in me the spirit of a trailblazer! He reminded me that the spirit of revival that was birthed in me could only grow. He told me that through faithfulness, obedience, persistence and a whole lot of Texas grit that I would see it. Now, you know I am a Texas girl – it had to come out!

God also challenged me: Did I want a series of revival meetings and everything that comes with that, or did I simply want Him? It was a very sweet time of developing intimacy with Him that is still growing to this day! He also taught me that through intimacy comes knowledge of who we are in Christ - our identity. This, in turn, enables us to walk in the God-given authority that we carry as believers.

Eugene Peterson's *Message Bible* sheds much light on this passage:

> **"Then I looked, and, Oh! - a door open into Heaven. The trumpet-voice, the first voice in my vision, called out, "Ascend and enter. I'll show you what happens next."**
> **- Revelation 4:1 MSG**

Let's look at a few highlights in this scripture:

### "Then I Looked, and Oh!"

Turn your eyes, focus on Jesus. He is our priority. He is our treasure. He is our reward. There's nothing better than Jesus. There are some of you reading this book that have never experienced an intimate relationship with Jesus. This would be the greatest treasure you would receive from reading this book. There are others of you that know Jesus as your Savior but you have never had the opportunity to know him as your best friend, lover of your soul and Lord of your life. There are others that simply can't get enough and want more of Him! I think that is all of us.

> *"When we come up to where He is, it's like being in a plane high up in the air, overlooking the land. We receive God's perspective."*

### "A Door Open Into Heaven"

Wow! Do we have access into Heaven? Of course we do! We are learning that the veil between heaven and earth is getting thinner as we see the day approaching, and the return of Jesus coming closer. God has given us divine access through the Holy Spirit in us.

> **"For as the waters fill the sea, the earth will be filled with an awareness of the glory of the Lord."**
> **- Habakkuk 2:14 NLT**

**"The Voice"**

"The Voice" is not just a TV show. This Voice is live and in living color. One of the most important pieces of our present Christian culture is understanding, knowing, and believing that God still speaks today, and He is speaking loud!

> **"But when the Father sends the Advocate as my representative—that is, the Holy Spirit—he will teach you everything and will remind you of everything I have told you." - John 14:26 NLT**

**"Come Up Here"**

We have the grand opportunity to come up to where Jesus is! He has invited us to His banqueting table! We come up to where He is through our worship, and through developing a relationship with Holy Spirit in our everyday lives.

**"I'll Show You What Happens Next"**

When we ascend to where He is, we have revelation, we see the way He sees, and we gain greater intimacy which gives us confidence, direction, and wisdom. As we ascend in worship, we also have the privilege of ministering angels that minister to and for us. We have divine access and direction. Holy Spirit is giving specific direction and order in this season.

**"Instantly"**

When we have His divine protocol, there is a quick work. We experience a suddenly. We learn to live in constant communion with the Father. Immediately, we are in the spirit and we experience true fellowship and intimacy.

> **"It was the Lord's Day, and I was worshiping in the Spirit. Suddenly, I heard behind me a loud voice like a trumpet blast." - Revelation 1:10 NLT**

There is nothing like a suddenly of intimacy. That voice that comes like a trumpet blast! That experience is where we might get the saying, "It is better caught than taught." When we come up to where He is, it is similar to being in a plane high up in the air, overlooking the land. We receive God's perspective. We receive direction. We receive Him.

*The Fruit of Intimacy*

As I stated earlier, our personal relationship and intimacy with Jesus are priority. Our relationship with Him is supreme, first, home base, our center, the beginning and the end. It will be our safe place when staying the course. By the way, the Trinity is three-in-one: Our Father, Jesus the Son and Holy Spirit. Each one has different functions and they work together. We have relationship with three-in-one. I refer to all three when talking about relationship and intimacy because all have a vital function in our Christian life. My desire for all of us is that we will begin to see in a greater way and learn to follow the thread of the Holy Spirit in our everyday lives as well as in seasons of standing, contending and staying the course.

My intimate relationship with Jesus has been in a constant growing cycle and I'm sure you would join me and say, "My plan is for that to never change!"

**"A man who is intimate with God will never be intimidated by man." - Leonard Ravenhill**

This quote is by the great preacher, author, and revivalist, Leonard Ravenhill, who lived in and is buried in our town of Lindale, Texas. It has stuck with me for many years, and through many experiences in life and ministry. There are dreams and desires that God has put in each one of us, that when spoken out loud can sound crazy and outlandish, and could cause us to feel intimidated by man and the world's system. Even the principalities of evil that rule over nations, regions, cities, churches and families can intimidate you into believing the lie that what God has promised you cannot come to pass, and is not possible. Intimacy with the Father, Son, and Holy Spirit will break that spirit of intimidation that rises against each one of us in the season of forging ahead for more.

Sometimes a new level of intimacy requires waiting on the Lord, waiting in His Presence, seeking Him with your whole heart. It's not always comfortable in our instant, "got to have everything at our fingertips" world. Pursuing Him for more is a wonderful, yet faith-filled experience. I have learned when going to a new level that there are many things along the way that Holy Spirit is teaching me. There are mindsets, belief systems, and just plain old lies that I need to come out of agreement with and change my mind.

One thing I do know is that He is a rewarder of those who diligently seek Him, and no good thing does He withhold from those who walk uprightly. Our Father loves to give good gifts. He will never turn away from us. In fact, He is overjoyed that we want more of Him because He wants more of us. He loves to be with us, to just hang out and enjoy life with us.

That was one mindset that changed for me. One day I heard the Father say to me, "You know, you don't always have to be working or accomplishing things in the Kingdom. I really like to just be with you. I like to spend time loving on you." Wow! What freedom, joy and peace came to me from that realization.

> *"'I heard the Father say to me, 'You know, you don't always have to be working or accomplishing things in the Kingdom. I really like to just be with you. I like to spend time loving on you.'"*

## *If I Could Just Sit for a While*

One of the most important things we can do is just learn how to sit for a while:

> *"If I could just sit for a while, I would tell You how much I love you, how grateful I am that You have changed my life and that You have redeemed my life. I would tell you that there's no other One like You. You bring life to my spirit, soul, and body. Thank You for saving me, dying for me, healing me, and setting me free. Once I was so caught up in life's worries but when I sit for a while, I lose all of that. I don't worry. I see things differently. You give me eyes to see the way You see, feel the way You feel. If I could just sit for a while, I would feel peace, contentment, joy and excitement, all at the same time. I can't get enough of You. I can't express adequately the way I feel. I don't know all the words. But I simply say, Thank you, I love you and so, could we just sit for a while? Yes, we sit."*

**"Arise, my love, my beautiful companion, and run with me to the higher place. For now is the time to arise and come away with me. For you are my dove, hidden in the split-open rock. It was I who took you and hid you up high in the secret stairway of the sky. Let me see your radiant face and hear your sweet voice. How beautiful your eyes of worship and lovely your voice in prayer.**

> You must catch the troubling foxes, those sly little foxes that hinder our relationship. For they raid our budding vineyard of love to ruin what I've planted within you. Will you catch them and remove them for me? We will do it together." - Song of Songs 2:11-15 Divine Romance
> The Passion Translation

## *Drink Deeply!*

> "With joy you will drink deeply from the fountain of salvation! In that wonderful day you will sing: "Thank the LORD! Praise his name! Tell the nations what he has done. Let them know how mighty he is! Sing to the LORD, for he has done wonderful things. Make known his praise around the world." - Isaiah 12:3-5 NLT

"Learning to drink deeply" is a theme of my life and ministry. I believe God is calling believers to live the true, Christian life in constant fellowship with Holy Spirit and drink, drink, drink! For too long, many Christians have lived on substitutes and counterfeits. They have never learned to drink freely themselves.

We have created a church culture that has not taught believers to eat of the Word of God and drink of the Spirit for themselves. God is calling for His Bride to mature and walk in the inheritance of being His sons and daughters who will drink from the Living Water of Life!

> **"Come!" say the Spirit and the Bride. Whoever hears, echo, "Come!" Is anyone thirsty? Come! All who will, come and drink, Drink freely of the Water of Life!" - Revelation 22:17 MSG**

## Chapter 2
## Winds of Change

"Are your ears awake? Listen. Listen to the Wind Words, the Spirit blowing through the churches. I'm about to call each conqueror to dinner. I'm spreading a banquet of Tree-of-Life fruit, a supper plucked from God's orchard."
- Revelation 2:7 MSG

I would say that one of the most challenging things in this whole process of learning to stay the course is also knowing when change is in the air. God is trying to get you on the right course for the right season. I do believe that there is a rhythm that we can learn through having a relationship with Jesus and the Holy Spirit for which we can learn the times and the seasons in our lives.

> **"For everything there is a season, a time for every activity under heaven." - Ecclesiastes 3:1 NLT**
>
> **"From the tribe of Issachar, there were 200 leaders of the tribe with their relatives. All these men understood the signs of the times and knew the best course for Israel to take."**
>
> **- 1 Chronicles 12:32 NLT**

If you have been alive for any length of time, you have had to go through change. It's probably one of the biggest reasons that people fail to attain their dreams and walk fully in their destiny. Some people love change. They love to rearrange their furniture in their homes. They are good with moving around or changing jobs and doing different things all the time. I have to say, I have not been one of those people. Once I get my furniture and things in place in my home I like it to stay put. I have no desire to improve upon what I know I like and already thought through.

> *"There is a rhythm that we can learn through having a relationship with Jesus and the Holy Spirit for which we can learn the times and the seasons in our lives."*

A fun joke that my husband Steven likes to play on me is to rearrange or move a decoration in our home. I know immediately if something has been even slightly moved and put it right back the way I had it. That is a casual example but many times we are such creatures of habit that we do not like to do things differently in our lives.

God has taught me so much in this area in a big, sometimes comical, way. Every time we had a baby, we would also move or buy a new vehicle, or something like that. We would be involved in a construction project in the church, and there would not be just one thing affected but many, with multiple projects going on at once. We would have leadership shifts or business changes all at once. I would say, "God, can't we just do one thing at a time in my orderly life my way, with no chaos?" Funny, but it's not always so.

Change usually involves much change. One time Steven printed out the phrase, "great change" and placed it all over our house. It helped us to embrace in the natural what God was doing in the spirit. Many times when God is ordering our steps and determining our course there is change and rearranging, not only of mindsets, but in our natural lives as well.

I have seen this process take place over and over in my life. The Lord starts speaking change and shift. I might think it's only spiritual, but He demonstrates it to me in my natural life. In the same way, we might hear the Lord speaking to us about change and we immediately think we are moving to another town. In reality, He is calling us to a higher level of thinking and shifting of mindsets. One might feel that moving, in the natural, is an easier task than changing our minds sometimes!

## "We can make our plans, but the LORD determines our steps." - Proverbs 16:9 NLT

The process of making our plans, yet allowing the Lord to determine our steps, is so very important in learning to stay the course. Through the years my husband and I have grown so much in learning this process. We are learning to recognize that we need to do something different when the Holy Spirit is blowing and moving, not only in our personal life but in ministry, also. Our constants are the Word of God, our relationship with Him, our marriage and family relationships, our community of fellowship and the call of God upon our lives.

> *"When Holy Spirit is blowing and change is in the air, we must be sensitive to that change and respond in obedience, no matter how uncomfortable it may feel."*

There are personal steps of faith that we have taken that would never have taken place if we were not listening to the winds of change, the spirit blowing. I believe it is crucial for the body of Christ to embrace winds of change in this season and to remember that His ways are higher than our ways.

We can stay consistent and still learn when the winds of change are breathing on a ministry, activity or event in our lives. When Holy Spirit is blowing and change is in the air, we must be sensitive to that change and respond in obedience, no matter how uncomfortable it may feel. Many times we keep pressing and pushing to make something work. It's like putting a square peg into a round hole. We keep doing the same things over and over just because that is more comfortable for us. Change is never comfortable. We like comfort. There is nothing wrong with that if we allow Holy Spirit to be our Comforter in the midst of change.

The best thing to do when change is in the air is to rest in the Lord. We must not enter into toil. That sounds polar opposite but I believe it is the Kingdom way! We must let God reorder what our season is supposed to look like. In the midst of change, you may have some "freak out" days, as we used to call them, when BIG change was happening and we had no grid for it. The best thing you can do is find your rest and comfort in Him.

> *"God is so pleased with our obedience to change that just the slightest movement results in the ripple effect we call breakthrough!"*

**"Those who live in the shelter of the Most High will find rest in the shadow of the Almighty. This I declare about the LORD: He alone is my refuge, my place of safety; he is my God, and I trust him." - Psalms 91:1-2 NLT**

Many times our motives for staying are good, but God has a better plan. We must be willing to lay down our ways of doing things, even our dreams, in order for God to redesign, remake, and remove, in order to make it better... make it His.

*"This is a new day, my daughter. Rejoice that I am restoring, renewing, reviving and remaking. This is a season of re-again, anew, over again, back."*

"Let Your hand be upon the man of Your right hand, upon the son of man whom You have made strong for Yourself. Then will we not depart from You; revive us (give us life) and we will call upon Your name. Restore us, O Lord God of hosts; cause Your face to shine [in pleasure, approval, and favor on us], and we shall be saved!" - Psalm 80:17-19 AMP

## *You Have Stayed Long Enough*

"When we were at Mount Sinai, the LORD our God said to us, 'You have stayed at this mountain long enough. It is time to break camp and move on. Go to the hill country of the Amorites and to all the neighboring regions—the Jordan Valley, the hill country, the western foothills, the Negev, and the coastal plain. Go to the land of the Canaanites and to Lebanon, and all the way to the great Euphrates River. Look, I am giving all this land to you! Go in and occupy it, for it is the land the LORD swore to give to your ancestors

**Abraham, Isaac, and Jacob, and to all their descendants." - Deuteronomy 1:6-8 NLT**

So, you are reading a book about staying the course and we have a section at the beginning that reads, "You have stayed long enough!" What is this about? Remember, it's so important that we stay the right course! The church has been in a season of stagnation. The word of the Lord to the body of Christ right now is that we have stayed long enough in our comfort, in our religion, and in our slumber. Our nation, and the nations of the world, have suffered because of our staying "long enough" in one place. It's time for believers to break camp out of tradition, move on, and go **to** the land. That's movement.

God is so pleased with our obedience to change that just the slightest movement results in the ripple effect we call breakthrough! Our faith pleases Him. He is calling us into our land and our inheritance. Many times we feel like we are the only person doing such a thing. That's okay. I tend to think God may allow this. We keep our eyes locked into His. We trust Him in all things.

**"The past events have indeed happened. Now I declare new events; I announce them to you before they occur." - Isaiah 42:9 HCSB**

**"Do not remember the past events, pay no**

> **attention to things of old. Look, I am about to do something new; even now it is coming. Do you not see it? Indeed, I will make a way in the wilderness, rivers in the desert."**
>
> **- Isaiah 43:18-19 HCSB**

It is so important during the season of change that we feed on the word of God and His faithfulness, and that we remain grateful for where we are and where we are going. Some people make everyone around them miserable when change is happening in their lives. They make the people, job, church and/or present town they are living in feel second rate, not good enough for them, or that something is wrong with it. That is an attitude and spirit that we must not carry in the season of change. There is no love or honor in that. We have said to our sons many times when they were moving into a new season in life, whether in school, in jobs or even in relationships, that it was so important how they ended a season. How we end a season can very well determine how we enter the next season of our lives. We transition and move in faith, love and in the strength of the Lord!

> **"The Lord turned to him and said, "Go in the strength you have and deliver Israel from the power of Midian. Am I not sending you?"**
>
> **- Judges 6:14 HCSB**

We must go in the strength we have! We don't need to have every detail figured out before we make a change. In fact, many times, our movement paves the way for each step we take. One time during a huge transition in our life and ministry, a wonderful missionary friend from Mexico gave me a word of encouragement. She said she saw me stepping into a forest of trees, which represented uncharted territory. As I stepped out, a stone would appear as I stepped onto it. With each step, a stone would appear under me leading in the direction that I needed to go. With each step came a greater confidence and joy that I was being led on the right path. The joy of the Lord is our strength!

> *"This change and movement must be embraced by the people of God in order to reach the lost and hurting in this world."*

**"What joy for those whose strength comes from the LORD, who have set their minds on a pilgrimage to Jerusalem." - Psalms 84:5 NLT**

**"And Nehemiah continued, "Go and celebrate with a feast of rich foods and sweet drinks, and share gifts of food with people who have nothing prepared. This is a sacred day before our Lord. Don't be dejected and sad, for the joy of the LORD is your strength!" - Nehemiah 8:10 NLT**

> "The LORD is my strength and shield. I trust him with all my heart. He helps me, and my heart is filled with joy. I burst out in songs of thanksgiving." - Psalms 28:7 NLT

*He's On the Move!*

> "Shout and celebrate, Daughter of Zion! I'm on my way. I'm moving into your neighborhood!" GOD's Decree. Many godless nations will be linked up with GOD at that time. ("They will become my family! I'll live in their homes!") And then you'll know for sure that GOD-of-the-Angel-Armies sent me on this mission. GOD will reclaim his Judah inheritance in the Holy Land. He'll again make clear that Jerusalem is his choice. Quiet, everyone! Shh! Silence before GOD. Something's afoot in his holy house. He's on the move!" - Zechariah 2:10-13 MSG

We have an incredible advantage as believers when we experience change in our life, in that our God is alive and moving and active! We must move with the winds of change because He is moving and progressing. Even His Word is active and alive. We are His inheritance and He has called us to move with Him.

He is on the move, always! It's our opportunity as believers to stay in sync with God and His ways. The world responds to movement. In fact, we are in a constant state of change in our world. It's nice to be in partnership with Holy Spirit change and movement. This change and movement must be embraced by the people of God in order to reach the lost and hurting in this world.

> *"I am taking you to a place of action, my daughter. A place of movement, moving in the Spirit and moving among the Body! I am bringing you closer to opening the doors that are there for you. All you will need to do is walk through them - doors of provision, doors of influence, doors of anointing, strategic doors that will order your steps in and through the next few years, doors of blessing, doors of presence. Begin to look for them, pray for them; for they are already there in the Spirit. Your praise will bring them closer so that you may walk through them. I am speaking very specifically these days so it is important that you continue to be attentive to My Word and My Ways and My Voice. Completion is coming. New days are coming."*

In 2007, there was a season of completion in ministry and a new season beginning in our lives. It was great change and took much faith to walk out but our eyes were on the lover of our souls. In 2008 we moved to Lindale, Texas to become the pastors of a local church that was over 100 years old. This church had transitioned from a Baptist church to a Bible church to a Spirit-filled church and was getting ready to change into a Revival church! The new season would have never happened for us if we had not been carried on the winds of change and been listening to the "wind words" blowing.

> *"As we step out in faith in a big way, our faith level grows in so many areas of our lives. One large physical or spiritual change can many times make way for a series of changes and breakthrough."*

God was so faithful to show His pleasure of our stepping out and being willing to change that He blessed me personally by confirming in fun little things along the way. We moved into a fairly new neighborhood on lot eight, our address ended in eight, the last four digits of our home phone were 7888, the church address ended in eight. The number eight, which is the number for new beginnings, was everywhere in our lives in 2008. God is so fun like that!

> *"My daughter, I long to live through a people who will trust Me, who will allow Me to work through them. I am calling you to allow Me to do that. I have called you to a unique place...a place of miracles, signs and wonders, a place of amazement, a place of safety, a place of joy and contentment. I am with you. Continue this journey in trust, hope and faith. Remember, I am able to do exceedingly, abundantly, above all you can ask or think, according to the power that is at work in you. That power is working in you, it is being turned on like a motor - engine with passion, fueled with by worship. I love you, My daughter and I am with you."*

Wow! These were such words of encouragement and comfort from Holy Spirit to me as I was going through a season of change, and He has given me many more since then.

I have found that as we step out in faith in a big way, our faith level grows in so many areas of our lives. One large physical or spiritual change can many times make way for a series of changes and breakthrough. Faith pleases God and makes room for growth and change. He is able, even in the midst of great change in our lives.

Ephesians 3:20 has become a life scripture for me:

> **"Now to Him Who, by (in consequence of) the [action of His] power that is at work within us, is able to [carry out His purpose and] do super-abundantly, far over and above all that we [dare] ask or think [infinitely beyond our highest prayers, desires, thoughts, hopes, or dreams]."**
> **- Ephesians 3:20 AMP**

# Chapter 3
# New Wine Skins

**"It was the best of times, it was the worst of times…" - Charles Dickens,** *A Tale of Two Cities*

As we live our lives to stay the course and move forward into the destiny that God has for us, transition will become a common factor in the process. God is fresh! His Spirit is always moving and we have the opportunity to "follow the thread", or flow, in the river of His Spirit.

There is a loud clashing of the old and the new. Hold on! It's not comfortable but we must trust our Father. In this season, we are developing a greater trust, and gaining a better understanding of His love, His affection and His full confidence in us. During this time we must be willing to be uncomfortable.

Sometimes the new offends our minds, our pride, our way of thinking and our emotions. When this happens, we can experience a good test to see if our spirit is leading. When we are submitted to our Father and His ways, we are willing to "hold on" through the discomfort, trusting His Ways are higher and knowing that we will come through with more freedom, discernment, glory, and love. In essence, we get a whole lot more of Him! Our container grows!

> *"When we are submitted to our Father and His ways, we are willing to "hold on" through the discomfort, trusting His Ways are higher and knowing that we will come through with more freedom, discernment, glory, and love."*

We must make sure that we do not reject the new that God is bringing into our life. There is great grace available for this season. We have the opportunity to embrace change through humility and resist blockage that would try to stop or stifle this process. We receive the new by faith. We must not be tempted to vacillate, or doubt in the dark what God has said in the light.

> **"These wineskins were new when we filled them, but now they are old and split open. And our clothing and sandals are worn out from our very long journey." - Joshua 9:13 NLT**

In 2012, our church in Lindale, Texas had been in great change and transition, so on 12.12.12 (Yes! The number of government!)

we changed the 108-year-old church name to Bethesda Church.

Earlier that fall we had traveled to Washington, D.C. on our yearly outreach to lead worship and participate in David's Tent there. One evening, our team attended another session just to wor-ship and soak together. There was an incredible worship team leading that night. The worship was great! The musicians were amazing. The songs were the latest songs being sung in the body of Christ. Everyone was happy and excited to be worshipping in a large tent on the Ellipse, a beautiful lawn behind the White House.

It was a magical night and I was miserable. I could not get into the worship at all. I was feeling irritated and unsettled. I was feeling a great clash in my spirit and even in the natural. I was uncomfortable and getting more irritated by the moment, because I thought I should be joining in with our team in receiving so much from the Lord and just loving the experience.

I kept asking the Lord, "What is wrong with me?" Then, as only we can do sometimes, I moved on from me and started thinking that maybe something was wrong with the praise team. I thought, "Maybe it's the worship team leading worship. Maybe it's them, and they have sin in their life, or something is not right with their team."

Yes, I add this to the story because it's so typical of us when God is doing something in us to want to point fingers, blame others and say they are the problem, to turn that yucky feeling onto others. Thankfully, I did not stop there but continued to pray and ask Holy Spirit what was happening. He was merciful to me and showed me that he was removing an old wine skin and preparing me for a new one.

**"I am like a cask of wine without a vent, like a new wineskin ready to burst!" - Job 32:19 NLT**

The clash was loud and difficult in my spirit. It almost hurt. I had many questions and felt like I was in no man's land. I had feelings of not belonging, being displaced and lost. It was pretty miserable. I remember praying that night, "Father, I trust you and I know that you have a plan. I know that your ways are higher than my ways and that this change will be for my good."

> *"I began to embrace the removing of old thought patterns, of religious ways and beliefs that I had held dear. I let God do His thing! He said He would remove the old wine skin so I just said "YES!" and let Him do it."*

I began to embrace the removing of old thought patterns, of religious ways and beliefs that I had held dear. I let God do His thing! He said He would remove the old wine skin so I just said "YES!" and let Him do it. He also reminded me why we get new wine skins:

**"And no one puts new wine into old wineskins.**

**For the wine would burst the wineskins, and the wine and the skins would both be lost. New wine calls for new wineskins." - Mark 2:22 NLT**

As I walked through this process, thankfully I was not alone. Steven was experiencing the same clash and change. We said to ourselves, "There's no way we are going to be miserable alone." So after we changed our church name on 12.12.12, we decided that our declaration and word for the year in our church in 2013 would be, "A New Wine Skin." How fun and how exciting!

This was not the case at all, however. We had perfect peace in the changing of our name, as did our leadership and congregation; however, as the old wine skin began to be removed it was one of the most difficult years of our ministry. People left the church, the finances decreased and it almost seemed like we were dying. The bank rejected the church for a small loan, even though they knew that we had a three-million-dollar property with hardly any debt. They said we were on a downward spiral and didn't want to help us. We felt like we were scary to ourselves and to the community! I say this with a comical tone, but also with truth.

> *"A simple definition of revival is His arrival. There are so many wonderful things that happen when He shows up. There is also a Heavenly alignment that takes place in us that can be messy from our earthly perspective, but necessary for the course."*

We continued to place a priority on God's Presence and

Goodness in our lives and in our church. We trusted the word of the Lord that this was going to be for our good. God literally took off the old wine skin in our lives and ministry and transitioned us into a new wine skin. We would never want to repeat that year, but we wouldn't trade it either. God did so much in us, through us, and for us that would carry us into the new. It now represents a precious season where we remember the sweet times of worship in our services and in our house of prayer, and at our home. Sometimes, all we could do in these times of worship was lay down before the Lord in silence, wait on Him, trust Him and most of all, love on Him.

In our attempt for new wine skins we want to move from the old to the new, but we must remember that God, His ways, and His Word never changes. Methods change, and culture changes, but we must stay true to His Word and what the Spirit is saying. As we throw out the old, sometimes we have to get rid of what God never intended for us to have, or do, in the first place. Attaining a new wine skin can bring much freedom into our lives. Our heart and spirit must stay linked up with what the Spirit is saying. This season of attaining a new wine skin will shake off what doesn't belong in the first place.

> **"Make sure that you do not reject the One who speaks. For if they did not escape when they rejected Him who warned them on earth, even**

> **less will we if we turn away from Him who warns us from heaven. His voice shook the earth at that time, but now He has promised, Yet once more I will shake not only the earth but also heaven. This expression, "Yet once more," indicates the removal of what can be shaken — that is, created things — so that what is not shaken might remain. Therefore, since we are receiving a kingdom that cannot be shaken, let us hold on to grace. By it, we may serve God acceptably, with reverence and awe, for our God is a consuming fire." - Hebrews 12:25-29 HCSB**

The shaking and the removing of old wine skins prepares us for new wine skins which hold the new. New, fresh wine represents fresh baptism of the Holy Spirit and with it brings new revelation for a new time and season. God is giving the Body of Christ new wine skins so that we will be a container for the new that is being poured out in this day.

*Revival is Messy*

> "The rains of revival are as messy as any we've seen on the evening news. They discover leaks in our homes and bring hidden debris out into the open. And in some situations, they have been

**known to bring division, much like a house that crushed into a sinkhole. Those who say revival does not bring conflict need to reread their Bibles. Both scripture and church history testify to the sometimes puzzling effect of rain. Rain in great portions simply overpowers whatever stands in its way."** - Bill Johnson

"Without oxen a stable stays clean, but you need a strong ox for a large harvest."
- Proverbs 14:4 NLT

The changing from old wine skins to new wine skins is a process of revival or awakening in our lives, personally as well as corporately. I have experienced both. As we desire to stay the course in our destinies, we certainly will experience the messiness of revival. A simple definition of revival is His arrival. There are so many wonderful things that happen when He shows up. There is also a Heavenly alignment that takes place in us that can be messy from our earthly perspective, but necessary for the course.

Here are five simple yet profound keys that will help us to navigate through this sometimes difficult and uncomfortable experience. I will add that this process is where many quit and give up. We do not like the discomfort to our feelings and emotions, and its offensiveness to our minds. We do not receive or give grace like we should. There can be strife in relationships when change is taking place. This can affect our marriages and our homes, our local churches and business partnerships.

**Five Revival Keys**

*Revival Key: Thankfulness*
> **"Let us enter His presence with thanksgiving; let us shout triumphantly to Him in song."**
> **- Psalm 95:2 HCSB**

When messy revival shows up, be thankful He has come. In the midst of God changing and rearranging our heart, will, and mind we must thank Him. It feels like surgery now but we must know that we will come through with victory on the other end.

> **"Lord my God, You have done many things— Your wonderful works and Your plans for us; none can compare with You. If I were to report and speak of them, they are more than can be told." – Psalm 40:5**

*Revival Key: Resist Offense*
> **"When Jesus had finished His charge to His twelve disciples, He left there to teach and to preach in their [Galilean] cities. Now when John**

**in prison heard about the activities of Christ, he sent a message by his disciples And asked Him, Are You the One Who was to come, or should we keep on expecting a different one? And Jesus replied to them, Go and report to John what you hear and see: The blind receive their sight and the lame walk, lepers are cleansed (by healing) and the deaf hear, the dead are raised up and the poor have good news (the Gospel) preached to them. And blessed (happy, fortunate, and to be envied) is he who takes no offense at Me and finds no cause for stumbling in or through Me and is not hindered from seeing the Truth."**

**- Matthew 11:1-6 AMP**

God allows our mind, will, and emotions to be offended in order to capture our heart. I have to say, it is so important that we remember this. Why did Jesus talk about resisting offense right after He told of all of the miracles that were happening? Shouldn't everyone have just been celebrating the blind seeing and the deaf hearing, and all of the wonderful miracles Jesus was performing? It's so true, though – when new and good things are happening we only see the negative, or when it's not "normal" for us, we question whether it's right or not. It is

*Revival Keys:*
- ☐ *Thankfulness*
- ☐ *Resist Offense*
- ☐ *Unity*
- ☐ *Humility*
- ☐ *Walk by the Spirit*

important for us to resist offense always, but especially when God is doing a deep and new work in our lives.

## *Revival Key: Unity*

> **"Therefore I, the prisoner for the Lord, urge you to walk worthy of the calling you have received, with all humility and gentleness, with patience, accepting one another in love, diligently keeping the unity of the Spirit with the peace that binds [us]. There is one body and one Spirit-just as you were called to one hope at your calling- one Lord, one faith, one baptism,"**
> — Ephesians 4:1-5 HCSB

Unity is a priority to God and we must let it be ours in the midst of messy revival. Remembering that God works with individuals differently, and at different times, is important. Let's not have an "us and them" mentality. That is a political spirit that wants to control and thwart the moving of the Holy Spirit. We must commit to unity that centers on God's presence, and that we are the family of God rather than our doctrine and our agreement on every little thing.

## *Revival Key: Humility*

> **"At about the same time, the disciples came to Jesus asking, "Who gets the highest rank in**

> **God's kingdom?" For an answer Jesus called over a child, whom he stood in the middle of the room, and said, "I'm telling you, once and for all, that unless you return to square one and start over like children, you're not even going to get a look at the kingdom, let alone get in. Whoever becomes simple and elemental again, like this child, will rank high in God's kingdom. What's more, when you receive the childlike on my account, it's the same as receiving me."**
>
> **- Matthew 18:1-2 MSG**

Remain a novice, a student, and teachable! If we will walk in humility, we can always be growing and changing. If I have the mindset that I have arrived and know everything there is to know about God and His ways, I will not be open to a new wine skin or messy revival. I want to come as a child and continue for the rest of my life to learn more of His ways. Humility is the character of Jesus. It is the opposite of pride and we know the God opposes the proud but gives grace, or favor, to the humble. (James 4:6)

### *Revival Key: Walk by the Spirit*

> **"I say then, walk by the Spirit and you will not carry out the desire of the flesh. For the flesh desires what is against the Spirit, and the Spirit**

**desires what is against the flesh; these are opposed to each other, so that you don't do what you want. But if you are led by the Spirit, you are not under the law. Now the works of the flesh are obvious: sexual immorality, moral impurity, promiscuity, idolatry, sorcery, hatreds, strife, jealousy, outbursts of anger, selfish ambitions, dissensions, factions, envy, drunkenness, carousing, and anything similar. I tell you about these things in advance-as I told you before-that those who practice such things will not inherit the kingdom of God. But the fruit of the Spirit is love, joy, peace, patience, kindness, goodness, faith, gentleness, self-control. Against such things there is no law. Now those who belong to Christ Jesus have crucified the flesh with its passions and desires. Since we live by the Spirit, we must also follow the Spirit. We must not become conceited, provoking one another, envying one another." - Galatians 5:16-26 HCSB**

This passage of scripture speaks for itself! There is freedom in walking by the Spirit rather than our flesh. When you received Jesus into your life, you also received the precious Holy Spirit. Holy Spirit is our teacher and guide to living life. Walking in the Spirit keeps us free of sin and living by the law, which is why

> *"As we embrace the new, the clash of the old will be a distant memory. We will not even recognize ourselves. This is true revival that brings transformation, that will bring reformation."*

Jesus came. The devil would love to keep us living under remnants of the law and sin; however, receiving a new wine skin is taking off those old things and putting on freedom. Freedom is, and should be, the M.O. (modus operandi or mode of operation which are habits) for the Believer.

These revival keys are significant markers to navigate forward into what the Lord begins to do in our lives when we invite Him in. These keys unlock the fullness of the Holy Spirit in our lives and prepare us to take off old wine skins that do not bear fruit in our lives.

While the process of getting a new wine skin is not comfortable or fun, it prepares us for the new wine! Having a new, fresh container for the new of what God is doing in this present move of God, and what is to come, is crucial for the church. This new wine skin will allow us to welcome the harvest of souls that is coming into the Kingdom of God. This new wine skin will cause us to think differently, act differently and serve differently.

As we embrace the new, the clash of the old will be a distant memory. We will not even recognize ourselves. This new wine skin will once again, as in the book of Acts, cause us to receive the fresh baptism of the Holy Spirit that is being poured out for us, and on us, in this day. This is true revival that brings transformation that will bring reformation. We will talk about that in a later chapter.

CAMILLA CHARLES

# Chapter 4
# Baptism of Love

It was during a Sunday morning worship service that I heard these words over and over, and spoke them out: "I'm giving you a baptism of love so you won't have time to judge!"

This came forth during a season of receiving a new wine skin as God developed our church into an apostolic center and a revival hub. Many people didn't understand the change that was taking place in each one of us, individually as well as corporately.

> *"I'm giving you a baptism of love so you won't have time to judge!"*

God was uprooting things in each of our lives to make way for the new. As a result, not having "church as usual" brought on much resistance and agitation as we made this adjustment to a new normal. It felt as if the whole world was against us, and I strongly felt the weight of that resistance and judgment coming down upon me personally.

As I heard those words and spoke them out with authority, my voice got stronger and stronger, but my body got weaker and weaker with the weight of the baptism of His fiery love. I entered into a euphoric state. I began to laugh and cry and jump and squeal with excitement! Yes, I said squeal, and I'm still letting out squeals to this day!

> *"Euphoric: characterized by or feeling intense excitement and happiness."*

Suddenly I was so intoxicated with the love of God that I couldn't imagine taking time to judge in that moment, or any after that, either. He continued to fill me up and baptize me with fresh love. He replaced my offense with a heart of compassion. I was so excited about my journey of love, I was able to release forgiveness much more quickly, and my mind was completely changed toward them.

By the way, one of the meanings of repent is to change your mind, or mindset. His love totally set me free from passing judgement, and it was such a beautiful thing! The result of receiving that baptism of love never stops. It should be a way of life for every believer. If you have not experienced that baptism of love, all you have to do is ask for it. It is available for every Jesus believer. He is Love and there is no condemnation.

> "So now there is no condemnation for those who belong to Christ Jesus." - Romans 8:1 NLT

In this present move of God, love must be our umbrella, our canopy.

> "He brought me to the banqueting house, and his banner over me was love."
> - Song of Solomon 2:4 NKJV

I can truly come to His banqueting table in the presence of my enemies, and eat from His table. I have a deep love for Him and I receive His great love for me. In return, I love others well, starting with my husband and family, my friends, the body of Christ, pre-Christians and even my enemies.

> "You prepare a feast for me in the presence of my enemies. You honor me by anointing my head with oil. My cup overflows with blessings."
> - Psalms 23:5 NLT

I'm so amazed as I experience God's great love, that sometimes I don't have words to say. My heart aches with affection for Him. His sweetness has been my cup of victory in times of death, failure and disappointment. His faithfulness has been my food in times of happiness, and He has taught me to live with great contentment. As I am learning to live with a continual baptism of love, I am finding that I love more deeply, release and forgive more quickly, and cover more. My canopy of love is quite big. His name is Jesus.

> **"I am the true grapevine, and my Father is the gardener. He cuts off every branch of mine that doesn't produce fruit, and he prunes the branches that do bear fruit so they will produce even more. You have already been pruned and purified by the message I have given you. Remain in me, and I will remain in you. For a branch cannot produce fruit if it is severed from the vine, and you cannot be fruitful unless you remain in me. "Yes, I am the vine; you are the branches. Those who remain in me, and I in them, will produce much fruit. For apart from me you can do nothing. Anyone who does not remain in me is thrown away like a useless branch and withers. Such branches are gathered into a pile to be burned. But if you remain in me and my words remain in you, you may ask for anything you want, and it will be granted! When you produce much fruit, you are my true disciples. This brings great glory to my Father. "I have loved you even as the Father has loved me. Remain in my love. When you obey my**

**commandments, you remain in my love, just as I obey my Father's commandments and remain in his love. I have told you these things so that you will be filled with my joy. Yes, your joy will overflow! This is my commandment: Love each other in the same way I have loved you. There is no greater love than to lay down one's life for one's friends." John 15:1-13 NLT**

Love is a distinguishing characteristic in this present move of God. Our love for God, and His love for us, in turn, causes us to love others well. This is what will help us stay the course in life. Love is an action, a state of mind and a matter of the heart. The thread of the spirit that I talk about following, in order to stay the course, is only activated in love. This love has kept me in life! This love has carried me in life! This love has sustained me in life! If you are alive, and I know you are since you are reading this book, then you can say along with me, "I need love. I need to give love and I need to receive love."

> *"Our love for God and His love for us, in turn causing us to love others well is what will help us stay the course in life."*

We need each other in this present move of God. God is putting great teams together to work side by side. Steven and I have not only been a team in our marriage and home, but we have also worked very closely in ministry as a team. I can tell you that if love had not been, and is still, our canopy, we would have given up on working so closely together a long time ago.

We started singing together and working in ministry together at my parents' church when I was 18. A few years later, in 1989, we got married. We are both strong, some may say, type-A personalities. I would be misleading you if I said it has always been one big, fun, adventurous party. It has, at times, been very challenging and difficult. Regardless, we know, had we not chosen to stay the course in our marriage first and then in our working relationship, we would not be able to work and flow so well together now.

We have worked as a team, side by side, learning to give and take, learning to not be sensitive, learning to honor and respect one another. We sing and lead worship together. We co-pastor our church together. We travel in ministry together. We have meetings together. We clean our house together. We shop together. We have built houses together. Yes, you read correctly - more than one house! We have fun together.

> *"God is putting incredible teams together who will serve one another, help one another and promote one another. They will cover one another and pray for one another."*

Most of all, we have raised our two sons together and now we treasure what we have in them, and in each other. Thank God that we did not choose to forfeit the "together" that makes us not just Steven, not just Camilla, but Steven and Camilla. I release the Father's great love over you in Jesus' Name to live under His canopy in your marriage, in your family, in your ministry, in your personal and business relationships, and in every person you encounter!

> *"I'm getting more and more glimpses in the spirit of victory, breakthrough, miracles, healings and revival as I pray today. Many things we are praying and believing for are so close and they intermingle so much with the Body of Christ. Now is not the time for the Body to disconnect. We need each other and our miracles will affect each other."*

## Koinonia

What is 'koinonia'? It sounds like an old hippie term, or a phrase the Charismatics were using in the 1970's, or maybe even a kind of Korean food. You might shrug it off, but first let's talk about what it means. Koinonia is fellowship which comes by the Holy Spirit, to invade us and cause us to love one another dearly. Koinonia is used in the following verses:

> *Koinonia - fellowship, intimate friendship, partnership, communion. Koinonia comes by the Holy Spirit to invade us and cause us to love one another dearly.*

**"But if we [really] are living and walking in the**

**Light, as He [Himself] is in the Light, we have [true, unbroken] <u>fellowship</u> with one another, and the blood of Jesus Christ His Son cleanses (removes) us from all sin and guilt [keeps us cleansed from sin in all its forms and manifestations]." - 1John 1:7 AMP**

"The amazing grace of the Master, Jesus Christ, the extravagant love of God, the intimate <u>friendship</u> of the Holy Spirit, be with all of you."
- 2 Corinthians 13:14 MSG

"God will do this, for he is faithful to do what he says, and he has invited you into <u>partnership</u> with his Son, Jesus Christ our Lord."
- 1 Corinthians 1:9 NLT

"We saw it, we heard it, and now we're telling you so you can experience it along with us, this experience of <u>communion</u> with the Father and his Son, Jesus Christ." - 1 John 1:3 MSG

The intimate friendship, or koinonia, of the Holy Spirit and true, unbroken fellowship with one another is the root of the "community" buzz word that we use. True koinonia is available for us as believers, and is essential in this present move of God. It's the

Bible way and I can give testimony that it works.

A critical, unbelieving spirit is born out of a feeling of hurt resulting from disappointment. Many people have been hurt and disappointed because the enemy has tried to extinguish authentic koinonia, but we are gaining wisdom in this area. We are not allowing the devil to rob us of this treasure as believers.

> **"If you are wise and understand God's ways, prove it by living an honorable life, doing good works with the humility that comes from wisdom. But if you are bitterly jealous and there is selfish ambition in your heart, don't cover up the truth with boasting and lying. For jealousy and selfishness are not God's kind of wisdom. Such things are earthly, unspiritual, and demonic. For wherever there is jealousy and selfish ambition, there you will find disorder and evil of every kind. But the wisdom from above is first of all pure. It is also peace loving, gentle at all times, and willing to yield to others. It is full of mercy and the fruit of good deeds. It shows no favoritism and is always sincere. And those who are peacemakers will plant seeds of peace and reap a harvest of righteousness." - James 3:13-18 NLT**

We need each other! As I stated earlier, God is putting incredible teams together in this present move of God. They will serve one another, help one another and promote one another. They will cover one another and pray for one another.

> **"Be prepared. You're up against far more than you can handle on your own. Take all the help you can get, every weapon God has issued, so that when it's all over but the shouting you'll still be on your feet. Truth, righteousness, peace, faith, and salvation are more than words. Learn how to apply them. You'll need them throughout your life. God's Word is an indispensable weapon. In the same way, prayer is essential in this ongoing warfare. Pray hard and long. Pray for your brothers and sisters. Keep your eyes open. Keep each other's spirits up so that no one falls behind or drops out."**
> - Ephesians 6:13-18 MSG

"Above all, put on love — the perfect bond of unity." - Colossians 3:14 HCSB

We have found that teams in ministry are the way to go. In our ministry at Bethesda, we are learning this daily. In some of our most difficult seasons as an apostolic church body, our love for

God, and for each other, has carried us through. It has created a beautiful bond of unity that is so precious to us now. There is a synergy that God is creating through His people. Two are better than one. Teams that learn to flow together in an apostolic covering will have greater impact, with supernatural ease and longevity in ministry.

In this present move of God, there are miracles and harvest that we will only see happen as many different spiritual streams come together. We will choose to go for the glory, the anointing, and the harmony that is released through our unity. In our town, we have a community called New Harmony. We have declared and prophesied through the years with many prophetic prayer teams over our land, that East Texas will be a place of new harmony! I declare that over your land as well.

> **"How wonderful and pleasant it is when brothers live together in harmony! For harmony is as precious as the anointing oil that was poured over Aaron's head, that ran down his beard and onto the border of his robe. Harmony is as refreshing as the dew from Mount Hermon that falls on the mountains of Zion. And there the LORD has pronounced his blessing, even life everlasting." - Psalms 133:1-3 NLT**

Unity is key! We have found ourselves in recent years having a greater desire for more and more unity in our ministry, in our relationships, and in the body of Christ. We love gathering together with other local church bodies and we have a passion for Kingdom community. As local pastors, in the beginning of our growing desire for unity some might have mistaken our motives, but God's heart is that we may be one.

**"I pray that they will all be one, just as you and I are one—as you are in me, Father, and I am in you. And may they be in us so that the world will believe you sent me." - John 17:21 NLT**

There is such an anointing that comes in unity. I want to encourage local pastors, business owners, and all who desire unity, especially where there has been disunity, to not give up. Stay the course in this Kingdom mandate. Humility and love will carry you through this process, and keep you from walking in discouragement and rejection.

Steven and I purposefully join in other local ministry events, and seek out Kingdom fellowship. Our church loves to host regular regional gatherings. Steven was offered the opportunity to lead our local minister's fellowship. With faithfulness and persistence, our spiritual community is growing in great friendship and unity.

This did not happen overnight. Many give up on this treasure of anointing just before they see the fruit. God has not given up on you and me. He gives grace to us to not give up on His plans and destiny for our lives, either, even when we are living in the "desert seasons" of life. This is the way God put it:

> "They found grace out in the desert, these people who survived the killing. Israel, out looking for a place to rest, met God out looking for them!" God told them, "I've never quit loving you and never will. Expect love, love, and more love! And so now I'll start over with you and build you up again, dear virgin Israel. You'll resume your singing, grabbing tambourines and joining the dance. You'll go back to your old work of planting vineyards on the Samaritan hillsides, And sit back and enjoy the fruit— oh, how you'll enjoy those harvests! The time's coming when watchmen will call out from the hilltops of Ephraim: 'On your feet! Let's go to Zion, go to meet our God!'" - Jeremiah 31:2-6 MSG

For many of us, as the above Scripture says, God has started over with us and He is building us up again. In the past season, broken relationships and divided congregations, full of betrayal and sorrow, have caused us to stop singing and

> *"In the past season, broken relationships, divided congregations full of betrayal and sorrow have caused us to stop singing and dancing. He is resuming our song and dance and placing us in a beautiful vineyard where we will enjoy the harvest that is coming into the Kingdom of God!"*

dancing. He is resuming our song and dance, and placing us in a beautiful vineyard where we will enjoy the fruit that is coming.

I believe a large part of the fruit from staying the course is the harvest that is coming into the Kingdom of God! The watchmen are arising, up on our feet, stronger than ever in unity. We are headed to Zion, the place of His presence and His authority, to meet with our God!

## Chapter 5
## Let's Cross Over

"After the death of Moses the Lord's servant, the Lord spoke to Joshua son of Nun, who had served Moses: "Moses My servant is dead. Now you and all the people prepare to cross over the Jordan to the land I am giving the Israelites. I have given you every place where the sole of your foot treads, just as I promised Moses. Your territory will be from the wilderness and Lebanon to the great Euphrates River — all the land of the Hittites — and west to the Mediterranean Sea. No one will be able to stand against you as long as you live. I will be with you, just as I was with Moses. I will not leave you or forsake you. Be strong and courageous, for you will distribute the land I swore to their fathers to give them as an inheritance. Above all, be strong and very courageous to carefully observe the whole instruction My servant Moses commanded you. Do not turn from it to the right or the left, so that you will have success wherever you go. This book of instruction must not depart from your mouth; you are to recite it day and night so that you may carefully observe everything written in it. For then you will prosper and succeed in whatever you do. Haven't I commanded you: be strong and courageous? Do not be afraid or discouraged, for the Lord your God is with you wherever you go." - Joshua 1:1-9 HCSB

We have learned that the process of staying the course involves change, movement, and mobility. For our destiny, and for our dreams, we are following the thread of Holy Spirit in our life. In this present move of God, we are gaining the strength and the courage to cross over into the promised land. God is raising up brave sons and daughters to walk in the treasure of revival and receive our inheritance.

> *"As we follow the thread of Holy Spirit in our life, for our destiny, for our dreams and in this present move of God, we are gaining the strength and the courage to cross over into the promised land."*

Remember, we live in this world, but we are not of this world.

We do not operate according to the world's system. As His people, organizations, corpor-ations and nations, we do not have to be dictated by the world around us, or by what is happening in government, cult-ure or society. We, as believers, have authority, the power of our prayer and agreement to see change take place. Transformation is not just a theory – it can happen.

Let's look at this scripture in Joshua. Starting in verse one it says, "After the death of Moses..." We must partner with the new! This is a new season, a new heavenly order. A new generation is about to receive their promised land. The Lord tells Joshua to prepare to cross over to the land that He is giving to him, and to the people, as their inheritance. He gives them a strategy, and reminds them of the territory He is giving them. God gives them authority, and reminds them of the generational blessing upon their lives.

More than one time in this passage of scripture, God tells them to be strong and courageous, giving them assurance that He is with them. The Lord tells them not to get distracted and not to look to the left or the right, so that they will have success wherever they go. He reminds them to both keep and to declare the Word of the Lord. He reminds them that when they do these things they will prosper and succeed in whatever they do. Wow! This sounds like a great vision statement, business plan and order of execution all wrapped into one.

**"Go through the camp and tell the people to get their provisions ready. In three days you will cross the Jordan River and take possession of the**

land the LORD your God is giving you." Then Joshua called together the tribes of Reuben, Gad, and the half-tribe of Manasseh. He told them, "Remember what Moses, the servant of the LORD, commanded you: 'The LORD your God is giving you a place of rest. He has given you this land.' Your wives, children, and livestock may remain here in the land Moses assigned to you on the east side of the Jordan River. But your strong warriors, fully armed, must lead the other tribes across the Jordan to help them conquer their territory. Stay with them until the LORD gives them rest, as he has given you rest, and until they, too, possess the land the LORD your God is giving them. Only then may you return and settle here on the east side of the Jordan River in the land that Moses, the servant of the LORD, assigned to you." - Joshua 1:11-15 NLT

As they prepare to cross over, God tells them to get their provisions ready. In this last season, there have been many in the body of Christ who have been called into a high level of kingdom finances. They have been getting their provisions ready to cross over. They will finance revival and awakening for territories, regions, and nations. They have been called to finance stadiums filled with people that will hear the Gospel and receive Jesus! They will finance new inventions, movies and entertainment that will reach the culture of our day for

Jesus, and for the Kingdom of God.

I, personally, know many that have sacrificed in their personal lives and businesses for the greater cause of Kingdom finance. They have risked reputation and have invested their own finances. They have been getting ready to cross over and inherit the land that God has given us in this present move of God.

I find it very interesting that the Lord reiterated to them what Moses had already commanded them - that God was giving them rest in the midst of bringing them into this land. Learning to rest spiritually, mentally, and physically is a crucial Kingdom mandate in this season.

In addition, the keys of sowing and generosity are at work here. Joshua tells them that their families can remain in the land given to them, but the "strong warriors, fully armed" must go and help the other tribes conquer, and inherit their land as well. God had a plan for ALL of them to cross over together. You and I are not only called to inherit our own land, but to help others conquer, and inherit their land and destiny as well. God has a plan for you to stay the course, not only for your life, but for others around you!

> *"You and I are not only called to inherit our own land but to help others conquer and inherit their land and destiny as well. God has a plan for you to stay the course not only for your life but for others around you!"*

Verse 14 says, "STAY with them until the Lord gives them rest, and until they, too, possess the land." I am quite convinced that many of us have forfeited staying, not only for our destiny, but for the destiny of our families, friends, and many others around us. We are called to be strong and courageous and not fear. If we stay the course, we will conquer and inherit our land!

God is calling us to cross over into our destinies, and in doing so, we will bring many along with us. My mindset changed when I realized that my advancement in the Kingdom was not just for my family, my ministry, or my church but for people all around me. I want the local church down the road to advance. I want other ministries to advance, and see promotion. If you are a business owner, your mindset should not only be for your own success, but for other businesses around you, as well. When I can truly rejoice in others' promotion, I will cross over with joy and freedom!

You might be saying to yourself, "This sounds great, but what does this look like? And how do we do this?" I believe it's different for all of us, yet there will be many key ingredients that empower us to cross over. Much of what we are crossing into is unknown. It's a new thing! It's a new way! Our faith must be in God, and God alone, to put all the pieces together. God is looking for men and woman who will take Him at His word, who will move, and just act.

> **"So do not throw away your confidence; it will be richly rewarded. You need to persevere so that when you have done the will of God, you will receive what he has promised. For, "In just a**

> little while, he who is coming will come and will not delay." And, "But my righteous one will live by faith. And I take no pleasure in the one who shrinks back." But we do not belong to those who shrink back and are destroyed, but to those who have faith and are saved."
>
> **- Hebrews 10:35-39 NIV**

There is something about stepping out, and stepping over, into a new season in life that is very exciting. The more we take steps of faith and not shrink back, the more we see God leading and guiding us. I have had to stretch myself in this area. I like a constant in my life. I like to know what's ahead, and I live by my lists. While I still use my to-do lists to get my work and tasks completed, I have learned not to live this way in the Kingdom. Taking risks and living by faith is much more exciting, because I get to see my wonderful Father come in on the scene, and orchestrate things that I never would have imagined. This process is very spiritual, and biblical, and is how we, as believers, should live.

> "Now these are the gifts Christ gave to the church: the apostles, the prophets, the evangelists, and the pastors and teachers. Their responsibility is to equip God's people to do his work and build up the church, the body of Christ. This will continue until we all come to such unity

**in our faith and knowledge of God's Son that we will be mature in the Lord, measuring up to the full and complete standard of Christ. Then we will no longer be immature like children. We won't be tossed and blown about by every wind of new teaching. We will not be influenced when people try to trick us with lies so clever they sound like the truth. Instead, we will speak the truth in love, growing in every way more and more like Christ, who is the head of his body, the church. He makes the whole body fit together perfectly. As each part does its own special work, it helps the other parts grow, so that the whole body is healthy and growing and full of love."**

**- Ephesians 4:11-16 NLT**

These five gifts are given to all believers to equip us to do works of service, build the church, and grow in our maturity in Christ. In the past season, there has been a restoring and building up of the five gifts. The western church has been very strong in the functions of evangelists, pastors and teachers; however, the apostles and prophets have been the scary group, making noise, and wearing a title with no real function. That wrong

> *"We need all the gifts to be fully activated in order to cross over. This is God's design, and yet the church has forfeited our inheritance because of misconception and wrong teaching of the gifts. Now is our season for the body of Christ to embrace all five gifts that Jesus gave to us."*

belief system has prevented us from taking territory and nations for the Kingdom. It has hindered us from walking in unity with one another, and has stifled our true intimacy with Father, Son and Holy Spirit.

The apostolic function sees the full picture; is family-oriented, and knows how to take territory for the Kingdom. The prophetic function is the listening ear, and as the mouthpiece of God, brings visions to life, commanding dead, dry bones to rise. We need all the gifts to be fully activated in order to cross over. This is God's design, yet the church has forfeited our inheritance due to misconception and wrong teaching of the gifts. Misuse of the gifts is no excuse to reject the Word of God. The church has been hindered, because we have not embraced these gifts. Now is our season for the body of Christ to fully embrace all five gifts that Jesus gave to us. We will cross over when we operate in the fullness of Christ's design.

> **"Now, dear brothers and sisters, regarding your question about the special abilities the Spirit gives us. I don't want you to misunderstand this. You know that when you were still pagans, you were led astray and swept along in worshiping speechless idols. So I want you to know that no one speaking by the Spirit of God will curse Jesus, and no one can say Jesus is Lord, except by the Holy Spirit. There are different kinds of**

spiritual gifts, but the same Spirit is the source of them all. There are different kinds of service, but we serve the same Lord. God works in different ways, but it is the same God who does the work in all of us. A spiritual gift is given to each of us so we can help each other. To one person the Spirit gives the ability to give wise advice; to another the same Spirit gives a message of special knowledge. The same Spirit gives great faith to another, and to someone else the one Spirit gives the gift of healing. He gives one person the power to perform miracles, and another the ability to prophesy. He gives someone else the ability to discern whether a message is from the Spirit of God or from another spirit. Still another person is given the ability to speak in unknown languages, while another is given the ability to interpret what is being said. It is the one and only Spirit who distributes all these gifts. He alone decides which gift each person should have." - 1 Corinthians 12:1-11 NLT**

There is a restoration of the spiritual gifts taking place. The Holy Spirit desires for all of these gifts to be in operation. As we learn to receive and operate in these spiritual gifts, we will be fully equipped to cross over, go into all the world and preach the Gospel. This crossing over is really just a return to Biblical living, and will create the tension needed for revival, transformation, and true reformation in our world.

CAMILLA CHARLES

## Chapter 6
## Generous Living

God is generous. We are called to live a life of generous living. If we are all honest, without Jesus in our lives, none of us have this character trait at our core. This chapter is not limited to our giving in just one way. As believers, there is no separation of how we give. We give our love. We give our finances. We give our time in our relationships, and investments into our churches and communities. We give by releasing healing, freedom, and life to everyone with whom we come into contact. Generosity is a key component of this multicolored, and multifaceted, move of God that we've talked about in earlier chapters.

> *"Generous (of a person): showing a readiness to give more of something, as money or time, than is strictly necessary or expected. Synonyms: liberal, lavish, magnanimous, openhanded, freehanded, bountiful, unselfish, ungrudging, free, indulgent."*

"To you who are ready for the truth, I say this: Love your enemies. Let them bring out the best in you, not the worst. When someone gives you a hard time, respond with the energies of prayer for that person. If someone slaps you in the face, stand there and take it. If someone grabs your shirt, giftwrap your best coat and make a present of it. If someone takes unfair advantage of you, use the occasion to practice the servant life. No more tit-for-tat stuff. Live generously. Here is a simple rule of thumb for behavior: Ask yourself what you want people to do for you; then grab the initiative and do it for them! If you only love the lovable, do you expect a pat on the back? Run-of-the-mill sinners do that. If you only help those who help you, do you expect a medal? Garden-variety sinners do that. If you only give for what you hope to get out of it, do you think that's charity? The stingiest of pawnbrokers does that. I tell you, love your enemies. Help and give without expecting a return. You'll never—I promise—regret it. Live out this God-created identity the way our Father lives toward us, generously and graciously, even when we're at our worst. Our Father is kind; you be kind."

- Luke 6:27-36 MSG

Well, if you are like me, this hits you right at your core. I believe God is raising up radical, generous believers that will love, and give, at all costs. Even though this scripture is telling us to love our enemies, we can also relate this to friendships, and covenant relationships, that have become enemies. Relationships lost, because they did not love one another with this kind of generous love.

I love verse 36. It says that we should live out this, "God-created identity." We are in God and God is Love. That's our identity. Now, this sounds really good on paper, but living it out day to day is another story. Just get in your car and drive to work. You will be challenged to love right away! However, I do want to encourage you that grace is available to love generously, and graciously. There have been times someone has said something to me that was very harsh or angry and I would just fumble at my response to them. Of course later, I would always think to myself, "I should've said *that* to them, then I really would have had a good comeback." It's in those times that I thank God for HIS generous grace that He released to me to keep my mouth shut. Obviously, none of us do that perfectly well all of the time, but we are growing in that kind of generous love.

> *"When we choose generous living, we have the grace to love others, and still hold on to the promises of God for our life."*

When we choose generous living, we have the grace to love others, and still hold on to the promises of God for our life. We are called to love generously. We are called to give generously. We must not get so focused on reaching our own goal that we become like the world and allow selfishness to take over. We must pour out His love and His glory! We have the opportunity to invest, and sow, into another's dream. When we live like that it breeds generosity, and prevents selfishness.

> **"Jesus sent his twelve harvest hands out with this charge: 'Don't begin by traveling to some far-off place to convert unbelievers. And don't try to be dramatic by tackling some public enemy. Go to the lost, confused people right here in the neighborhood. Tell them that the kingdom is here. Bring health to the sick. Raise the dead. Touch the untouchables. Kick out the demons. You have been treated generously, so live generously.'" - Matthew 10:5-8 MSG**

This scripture in Matthew 10 is one of my life verses. When I think of all that Jesus has done in my life, I can't help but want to give it out! We can't lose when we live as Jesus did. I can testify that this kind of generous living has changed my life! I have learned that loving on people, and releasing the Kingdom, wherever I go is a fun adventure to take with the Lord.

While I'm not a fan of grocery shopping, I have had some of

the most amazing times loving on people at the supermarket. One day I prayed for a lady on an oxygen machine. I told her that God had highlighted her to me and He just wanted to love on her. I asked if I could pray for her health, and for her family.

As I began to pray, she immediately sensed a difference in her breathing. She felt lighter, and so much joy rose up in her heart, that she began to laugh. Her sister was there with her, and it turned out that they had just lost their mother the day before. God not only healed this lady, He released joy and comfort to both of them in a season of mourning. They felt so loved by their Heavenly Father that day.

> *"Jesus released Holy Spirit the Comforter to that lady and her family with tears flowing from all of us and love being poured out in waves and waves. That day the supermarket was my favorite place to be! I couldn't imagine being anywhere else on the planet."*

On another occasion, we were on a day of outreach with a team from our church. We had prayed before we left that God would highlight those He wanted to love on. Several of us walked to the back of the store, and saw a group of ladies shopping together. One lady just stood out to me. I looked right at her and said, "God loves you so much today. We've been walking around, knowing that He wanted to give something out today, and you are the one!" She looked right at me with amazement, somewhat stunned, but anxiously awaiting what was to come.

We began to prophesy over her, and speak the words of Jesus to her. Within moments, this lady collapsed into tears. We found out from a family member that she had just buried her 16-year-old son the day before. As we ministered to her, Jesus released Holy Spirit the Comforter, with tears flowing from all of us, and love being poured out in waves and waves. That day the supermarket was my favorite place to be! I couldn't imagine being anywhere else on the planet.

We can't go wrong loving on people and releasing the Kingdom! I could go on with testimonies of lives changed and healed at parks, coffee shops, the mall, and airports. We don't do these things with motives to make ourselves look better, or feel better, although you can't help feeling the Father's pleasure when His sons and daughters release love and healing. We don't even do these things to grow our churches when we go as a team, although many times they end up asking us what church we are from. We simply go to love and give generously.

> **"Peter and John went to the Temple one afternoon to take part in the three o'clock prayer service. As they approached the Temple, a man lame from birth was being carried in. Each day he was put beside the Temple gate, the one called the Beautiful Gate, so he could beg from the people going into the Temple. When he saw**

Peter and John about to enter, he asked them for some money. Peter and John looked at him intently, and Peter said, 'Look at us!' The lame man looked at them eagerly, expecting some money. But Peter said, 'I don't have any silver or gold for you. But I'll give you what I have. In the name of Jesus Christ the Nazarene, get up and walk!' Then Peter took the lame man by the right hand and helped him up. And as he did, the man's feet and ankles were instantly healed and strengthened. He jumped up, stood on his feet, and began to walk! Then, walking, leaping, and praising God, he went into the Temple with them. All the people saw him walking and heard him praising God. When they realized he was the lame beggar they had seen so often at the Beautiful Gate, they were absolutely astounded! They all rushed out in amazement to Solomon's Colonnade, where the man was holding tightly to Peter and John."

- Acts of the Apostles 3:1-11 NLT

I love that, in this story, the man born lame was at the gate called "Beautiful". When this healing took place, Peter and John were on their way to a prayer service. God is calling believers to live in constant fellowship with Him, and see prayer as a way of life. God is restoring us to Kingdom life!

Although Peter and John didn't have any money that day, they gave what they had. They gave him something much better than money – they gave him Jesus. They gave him healing. We are called to give what we have.

So many times, we think we have to wait until we have our lives all together to start giving or helping people, but that is not a Kingdom principle. If you have Jesus in your life, then you *always* have something to give. Always!

The amazing thing about living generously is, the more we give, the more we receive. I have experienced seasons of lack emotionally, physically and financially in my life. All of us are tempted to conserve what we have in those seasons, but life in the Kingdom teaches us to give at all times. Learning to stay the course and not give up in seasons of lack is crucial. Giving is our key to breakthrough. It will keep us on our set course.

> *"Life in the Kingdom teaches us to give at all times. Learning to stay the course and not give up in seasons of lack is crucial. Giving is our key to breakthrough. It will keep us on our set course."*

**"So let's not get tired of doing what is good. At just the**

right time we will reap a harvest of blessing if we don't give up." - Galatians 6:9 NLT

"The generous will prosper; those who refresh others will themselves be refreshed."
- Proverbs 11:25 NLT

*Prepare to Enlarge*

"'Sing, O childless woman, you who have never given birth! Break into loud and joyful song, O Jerusalem, you who have never been in labor. For the desolate woman now has more children than the woman who lives with her husband,' says the LORD. 'Enlarge your house; build an addition. Spread out your home, and spare no expense! For you will soon be bursting at the seams. Your descendants will occupy other nations and resettle the ruined cities.'" - Isaiah 54:1-3 NLT

This is an incredible word for the body of Christ! We are preparing for the coming harvest in this present move of God. It's time for another wave of revival and we are preparing to give birth. Everything we do in the Kingdom happens first in the spirit through the word of the Lord. That prophetic word prepares our hearts, our mindsets and our Kingdom activity. "Kingdom activity" means that our lives are supernaturally natural, and naturally supernatural. Our lives are called to mirror the Kingdom!

The Lord is calling His sons and daughters out of barrenness and into fruitfulness. If you feel that you have not been fruitful in your life and ministry, the season to birth is now coming for you. We are called to enlarge, and to prepare to inhabit the nations!

If you have ever had a new baby in your home, or have had friends and family preparing for a baby, you know there is a lot of STUFF to get. That less-than-10-pound baby takes over the house! When Steven and I had our babies, we were also traveling in ministry. We had a minivan, mostly for all the baby stuff that was needed. We spared no expense for what our babies needed. God is calling the church to enlarge our hearts, and mindsets, for His Kingdom and the coming harvest.

> *"In order to stay the course, we must remember God's timing is perfect. We learn to delight in His ways and not put unnecessary pressure on ourselves. We cannot compare our lives with others. We must stay our course, stay in the race and not give up."*

**"'Fear not; you will no longer live in shame. Don't be afraid; there is no more disgrace for you. You will no longer remember the shame of your youth and the sorrows of widowhood. For your Creator will be your husband; the LORD of**

**Heaven's Armies is his name! He is your Redeemer, the Holy One of Israel, the God of all the earth. For the LORD has called you back from your grief — as though you were a young wife abandoned by her husband,' says your God."**

- Isaiah 54:4-6 NLT

The Lord is telling us not to fear. He is removing shame and disgrace. Many of us have experienced these, due to dreams and callings that have not yet been fulfilled. We have felt like we had a big vision, yet have nothing to show for it. We have faced hope deferred in our hearts, because of the lack of fruitfulness. That shame and disgrace has affected our lives, and even caused physical sickness and depression.

The Lord is removing the grief and sorrow of the past. Only He can supernaturally do that. I have chosen, over and over, to not walk in, or partner with, shame, disgrace, sorrow or grief with regard to the success, or timing, of my life, ministry and career. Many have said that the region where we live is spiritually barren of revival and renewal. At times, we have felt shame and disgrace over that. In order to stay the course, we must remember God's timing is perfect. We learn to delight in His ways, and not put unnecessary pressure on ourselves. We cannot compare our lives with others. We must stay our course, stay in the race, and not give up.

> "'For a brief moment I abandoned you, but with great compassion I will take you back.... Just as I swore in the time of Noah that I would never again let a flood cover the earth, so now I swear that I will never again be angry and punish you. For the mountains may move and the hills disappear, but even then my faithful love for you will remain. My covenant of blessing will never be broken,' says the LORD, who has mercy on you." - Isaiah 54:7, 9-10 NLT

We have a covenant of blessing from the Lord upon our lives as believers. In this present move of God, recognizing and walking in our covenant is crucial.

> "'O storm-battered city, troubled and desolate! I will rebuild you with precious jewels and make your foundations from lapis lazuli.... I will teach all your children, and they will enjoy great peace. You will be secure under a government that is just and fair. Your enemies will stay far away. You will live in peace, and terror will not come near. If any nation comes to fight you, it is not because I sent them. Whoever attacks you will go down in defeat.'" - Isaiah 54:11, 13-15 NLT

Wow! What a covenant we have. What a declaration to speak over your life, your family, your city, your region, and your nation! We are in a season of rebuilding our nation, the Church, and our lives. I'm so glad that the last verse of this chapter ends with a victorious reminder.

**"But in that coming day no weapon turned against you will succeed. You will silence every voice raised up to accuse you. These benefits are enjoyed by the servants of the LORD; their vindication will come from me. I, the LORD, have spoken!" - Isaiah 54:17 NLT**

In our journey, we will have weapons of abandonment, confusion, helplessness, and a whole list of others thrown at us; but be reminded, and encouraged, that those weapons formed against us will not succeed. This is our benefit package as a believer!

CAMILLA CHARLES

## Chapter 7
## Wide Open Spaces

This may be one of my favorite parts of this book. As I already stated, I'm a Texas girl, and I love the wide-open spaces of our land where we live. We call it the rolling hills of East Texas. One of Steven's and my favorite activities is riding in our convertible along the winding county roads, going a bit fast, enjoying the wide-open land that is so green and luscious, when it rains.

He's the car guy, but I'm the horse girl. Even though I enjoy riding in that convertible, I love riding a horse in those wide-open spaces. I love the outdoor land. I love the sound of the trees blowing in the breeze, the birds chirping and the farm dogs barking. I love the smell of the leather, and even the other smells that come with it. I love sitting up high on a well-trained horse, one that knows how to follow the gentle nudge of the bit, even perceives your confidence and mood, to know when to pick up the pace.

I love walking and trotting in the wide-open spaces. I am not as confident yet in loping and running, but I am choosing to stay the course in that area. I am blessed to have some barrel racing champions in our church, and as friends, so they are helping me.

Although I am not running on a horse in the natural, yet, God knows me and loves me. Many times my Heavenly encounters with Him are on a horse. Together we run as fast as we can go through the wide-open spaces, up and down the hills, going for miles across the open plain. It's what I do with Him in my free time. I run with no restraints, often bareback, holding on to the mane laughing and breathing in the fresh air.

> *"God is taking us into a spacious place in the Kingdom! In this last season, many of us have been re-digging the wells of revival, believing and contending for this present move of God."*

This is a picture of my great trust in Jesus, our relationship, our intimacy, and the fun and freedom that I have in Him. It's also an exhilarating feeling of conquering the land! God wants that for each one of us. You might be in a fast little convertible racing down the highway, or in an airplane flying across the wide-open lands. Whatever it may be, God wants to take you, and me, into a spacious place in our heavenly encounters with Him!

> "Dear, dear Corinthians, I can't tell you how much I long for you to enter this wide-open, spacious life. We didn't fence you in. The smallness you feel comes from within you. Your lives aren't small, but you're living them in a small way. I'm speaking as plainly as I can and with great affection. Open up your lives. Live openly and expansively!"
>
> - 2 Corinthians 6:11-13 MSG

God is taking us into a spacious place in the Kingdom! In this last season, many of us have been re-digging the wells of revival, believing and contending for this present move of God. Along the way we may have encountered some other wells, such as the following story in the Bible, but get ready, the Lord has been making room for us in our cities, regions and nations. We are entering in to a season of fruitfulness!

> "When Isaac planted his crops that year, he harvested a hundred times more grain than he planted, for the LORD blessed him. He became a very rich man, and his wealth continued to grow. He acquired so many flocks of sheep and goats, herds of cattle, and servants that the Philistines became jealous of him. So the Philistines filled up all of Isaac's wells with dirt.

These were the wells that had been dug by the servants of his father, Abraham. Finally, Abimelech ordered Isaac to leave the country. 'Go somewhere else,' he said, 'for you have become too powerful for us.' So Isaac moved away to the Gerar Valley, where he set up their tents and settled down. He reopened the wells his father had dug, which the Philistines had filled in after Abraham's death. Isaac also restored the names Abraham had given them. Isaac's servants also dug in the Gerar Valley and discovered a well of fresh water. But then the shepherds from Gerar came and claimed the spring. 'This is our water,' they said, and they argued over it with Isaac's herdsmen. So Isaac named the well Esek (which means "argument"). Isaac's men then dug another well, but again there was a dispute over it. So Isaac named it Sitnah (which means "hostility"). Abandoning that one, Isaac moved on and dug another well. This time there was no dispute over it, so Isaac named the place Rehoboth (which means "open space"), for he said, 'At last the LORD has created enough space for us to prosper in this land.'"

- Genesis 26:12-22 NLT

I am always encouraged by this story in the Bible. This word came alive to me in 2008 when we first became pastors in Lindale. It consumed me for a season, as so many times the Word of God can do. At prayer meetings, we would run this entire chapter across our media screen and thank God for the open spaces in our land. We prayed to re-dig the wells of revival in our land and region.

In our little town we are blessed to have had great men and women of God such as Leonard Ravenhill, David Wilkerson, Steve Hill, Keith Green, and Winkie Pratney reside here with their ministries; some are even laid to rest here. Ministries such as Youth With A Mission, Teen Challenge Teen Mania, World Challenge,

> *"Many of you will identify that you have walked (or you are still walking!) through this season but will start believing that your wide-open spaces are still to come. You will not stop short but you will keep digging!"*

Mercy Ships, Last Days Ministries, and many more have all been based out of our small, yet wide-open, space. These are just a few names, not to mention the many from our larger town of Tyler and our East Texas region, which would include R.W. Schambach, Larry Lea and Chuck Pierce. Wow! That's a deep well with which we are so grateful and honored to be connected and yet we know there is still more for our region; and not just our region but the nations that our region will affect.

Religion, complacency, and compromise have been the dirt that has stopped up our wells. Thankfully, throughout the years, God has placed faithful intercessors and those that would believe, not give up and stay the course, for the best is still yet to come.

As you read this chapter, my prayer is that many of you will identify that you have walked, or you are still walking, through this season; however, that you will start believing that your wide-open spaces are still to come. You will not stop short but you will keep digging! Some of you reading this have already come into your wide-open spaces. You have been faithful, you have not quit and you are already walking in a wide-open, spacious place, but get ready ... there is still more to come!

Remember that when Isaac began digging to reopen the wells, he had already planted crops, and was a wealthy man. In fact, the Philistines became jealous of him, and filled up his wells with dirt. They asked him to leave. They were intimidated by him. Many of us have had fruitful lives, yet we know there is more. Revival is just that. It's more of God. It's the fullness of the Spirit of God.

> *"Argument: an exchange of diverging or opposite views, typically a heated or angry one. Synonyms: disagreement, quarrel, squabble, fight, dispute, wrangle, clash, altercation, feud, contretemps, disputation, falling-out."*

We desire to stay the course for our full inheritance, but the enemy has released spirits of intimidation and jealousy against us. Many of us have dug wells. We have placed our stake in the ground. We have claimed our land and territory. Like Isaac, we have also changed the name of our region. It has been said of East Texas for many years that it's "a hard place" spiritually. We have changed that declaration to, "An open heaven and a portal for the glory of God." We have come into agreement with what God says over our region and we have kept digging. We have chosen to come into agreement with our God-given spiritual DNA, and our divine spiritual destiny.

There is not much description needed for the first two wells but we will look at them briefly. Isaac named the first well "argument." The second well was named "hostility." I think many of us could say that we have been at these wells at times in our lives. The wells of argument and hostility have tried to thwart many in the body of Christ. These wells have broken up marriages and families. They have caused altercations and breaches in businesses. These wells have split churches, and divided covenant relationships. They have kept regions of pastors and churches from getting along, and worshipping together, and working together to successfully reach their cities for the gospel of Christ. Spiritual streams have been in opposition and competition with one another. These wells have kept organizations from working together to reach the nations!

> *"The Lord has heard our cry for revival and awakening in our land. He is opening a new well called Open Spaces! It's a spacious place. He is our warrior and He is fighting for us. He is our help and support in the time of need."*

Yet, I love this scripture from one of the darkest and most challenging books of the Bible:

**"I know that You can do anything and no plan of Yours can be thwarted." - Job 42:2 HCSB**

Let's look at verse twenty-two from the passage in Genesis that says, "Abandoning that one, Isaac moved on and dug another well." I'm so glad that he did not stop after digging the wells called argument and hostility! My friend, we can't either! We must KEEP DIGGING!

This entire book hinges on this one thing. The church has forfeited our nation, the nations of the world, our regions, our cities, our churches, our marriages and families. We have even given up on ourselves in areas that still need growth and development. We must get back in the race! We must pick up our shovels and dig again!

**"I called to the Lord in distress; the Lord answered me and put me in a spacious place."**
**- Psalms 118:5 HCSB**

The Lord has heard, and is hearing our prayers for more! He has heard our cry for revival and awakening in our land. He is opening a new well called, "Open Spaces"! It's a spacious place. He is our warrior and He is fighting for us. He is our help and support in the time of need. He sees the condition of the United States and He is ready to rescue us because He has delighted in us.

> "He rescued me from my powerful enemy and from those who hated me, for they were too strong for me. They confronted me in the day of my distress, but the Lord was my support. He brought me out to a spacious place; He rescued me because He delighted in me. For I have kept the ways of the Lord and have not turned from my God to wickedness."
> - Psalms 18:17-19, 21 HCSB

We have an opportunity to stand in the gap, raise up the sword and fight for our land. God is calling us to keep His ways, turn away from wickedness and see the nations saved! God is merciful and kind and He does not desire to hand us over to the enemy. I want to speak directly to YOU and tell you that our Heavenly Father does not desire to hand YOU over to the enemy. He has been with you through devastation and loss. He has been with you through sickness, and even death. So, now, make your declaration, saying, "He has set my feet in a spacious place!"

> "I will rejoice and be glad in Your faithful love because You have seen my affliction. You have known the troubles of my life and have not handed me over to the enemy. You have set my feet in a spacious place." - Psalms 31:7-8 HCSB

I love the following verse from the Message Bible. I get the picture of many being trapped in religion, and in bondage to sin, but God setting people free, to leap and sing with abandon like children. In a humorous way, I also can't help but think it's like unbuttoning your favorite pair of jeans that you were determined to wear, even though they were too tight, and you finally get home and cry aloud, "I need room to breathe!"

> **"I hate all this silly religion, but you, GOD, I trust. I'm leaping and singing in the circle of your love; you saw my pain, you disarmed my tormentors, You didn't leave me in their clutches but gave me room to breathe."**
> **- Psalms 31: 6-8 MSG**

God's Word is key to setting us in a spacious place. God's Word is key to keeping us in a spacious place.

> **"I will walk freely in an open place because I seek Your precepts." - Psalms 119:45 HCSB**

> **"I will walk in freedom, for I have devoted myself to your commandments." - Psalms 119:45 NLT**

In Genesis 26:22, Isaac moved on and dug another well. This time there was no dispute over it. Yes! This time is now. The Lord has created enough space for us to prosper in the land. We serve a creative God, who has made a space uniquely for each of us, to walk in our inheritance, and fulfill our destinies. My prayer for us is that we will ride with the One called Faithful and True on that white horse of Victory! We will stay our course, and charge through, until we cross the finish line into our wide-open spaces!

> **"Lord, You are my portion and my cup of blessing; You hold my future. The boundary lines have fallen for me in pleasant places; indeed, I have a beautiful inheritance."**
>
> **- Psalms 16:5-6 HCSB**

# Chapter 8

# Yellow Walls, Butterflies and Fives

I love to meditate on the Word, God's Promises, and prophetic words spoken to me personally. I have filled this book with His precious promises that have meant a great deal to me throughout my journey of staying the course. Nevertheless, of all of the things that I am believing and dreaming to accomplish with the Lord, my most important pursuit is intimacy and relationship with Him.

The deepest part of my being longs after connection with Father, Son and Holy Spirit in this life, and for eternity. I believe to my core that He is always with me, always for me, and always loving me, more deeply than I can ever imagine. My highest and first priority is knowing Him, and being found in Him. Too many people have run the race, to win in life, in relationships, in ministry, or in business, and have allowed their relationship with Jesus to fall low on their list of priorities.

> "But everything that was a gain to me, I have considered to be a loss because of Christ. More than that, I also consider everything to be a loss in view of the surpassing value of knowing Christ Jesus my Lord. Because of Him I have suffered the loss of all things and consider them filth, so that I may gain Christ and be found in Him, not having a righteousness of my own from the law, but one that is through faith in Christ — the righteousness from God based on faith. My goal is to know Him and the power of His resurrection and the fellowship of His sufferings, being conformed to His death, assuming that I will somehow reach the resurrection from among the dead." - Philippians 3:7-11 HCSB

This intimacy with the Lord is my first — my home base, my safe place, my highest joy, my deepest river. It's the place I was created to dwell in and live. It's the place where I am most comfortable. It's where I pour out my heart with tears of gratitude, questions and even frustrations. It's the place where He speaks to me, loves on me and comforts me. The ministry of the Holy Spirit is life changing, and is my anchor in times of crashing storms, that would otherwise cause me to drown!

One of my life scriptures is from the book of Song of Solomon. It is a love story, full of passion and fiery love.

> "Set me like a seal upon your heart, like a seal upon your arm; for love is as strong as death, jealousy is as hard and cruel as Sheol (the place of the dead). Its flashes are flashes of fire, a most vehement flame [the very flame of the Lord]!"
>
> - Song of Solomon 8:6 AMP

I have a lovely sitting area in my bedroom painted in a beautiful, bright and cozy yellow. I love my fellowship time with the Lord in that room surrounded by vibrant color. It's a place for intimacy, meditating and dreaming, where I love on Him, and He loves on me. In those times, He pursues me. He heals my physical and emotional wounds. He assures me that everything is going to be all right. He reminds me of His Word - that He is the same, yesterday, today, and forever. He reminds me that He is not a man that He would lie or change His mind.

> *"Meditating, soaking, breathing in God's presence and waiting on Him is one of my highest joys in life! It is where I am complete. Even if I come in feeling low, despondent, helpless and discouraged or physically tired, I come out with renewed vision, strength, encouragement, peace and assurance from and in Him"*

> " God is not a man who lies, or a son of man who changes His mind. Does He speak and not act, or promise and not fulfill? I have indeed received a command to bless; since He has blessed, I cannot change it." - Numbers 23:19-20 HCSB

I love my time with Jesus! He comes into my room with assurance and releases joy. Holy Spirit comes as the Comforter, going to my deepest parts, the depths of my spirit, soul, and body. It is in that place that tension, stress, pain, hurts, wounds, unbelief, doubt, fear (and the list goes on) has to leave. Meditating, soaking, breathing in God's presence and waiting on Him is one of my highest joys in life! It is where I am complete.

Even if I come in feeling low, despondent, helpless and discouraged, or physically tired, I come out with renewed vision, strength, encouragement, peace and assurance from, and in, Him. I find the joy of God-encounters and going into the third heaven exhilarating! Many Christians don't believe they can have encounters – they think it's just for people in the Bible or something that happened to people from another time in history.

I have had many wonderful encounters, but there is one in particular I want to share. I was with Jesus, and we were in a very small garden in a safe place. Jesus gave me a big hug and said, "It's going to be okay, you can do this." We ran through a maze that was built to be an adventure. We admired, and smelled, some beautiful flowers. Then we ran some more through this fun maze adventure. At one point Jesus just looked at me and put his hand on my face – just as if He was so proud of me and so happy to be with me.

We continued to run and we came out into a wide-open space. There was a beautiful brown horse! We hopped on quickly, and took off, flying into the wide-open green pastures, rolling hills, and open spaces that I love! The weather was clear, crisp and cool, and there were no limits, so we ran really fast on this brown horse. Next, we took

> *"As I have continued to stay the course, I have become much more aware of the supernatural ways of our Father and His Kingdom. His goodness and faithfulness has been on display in many ways, both large and small."*

some time at the home-base to be with the Father. I sat in His lap, and He worked on my heart a bit, sewing it up and putting some plaster-healing ointment on it. Holy Spirit came in, and wrapped a white and silver material around me.

Father, Son, and Holy Spirit were all talking back and forth, discussing what to give me, and how to take care of me. Jesus and the Father were both taking care of me, while Holy Spirit was swirling around me. The Father began to heal some hurts, and puncture wounds, that I had received. He gave me a stronger, heavier armor and a new mantle that would provide some protection for this season. My heart received some surgery and TLC. They ministered to me and took care of me as a daughter, warrior, friend, family member, and 'sent one'.

I share this with you to encourage you that you can have Heavenly encounters as well. If you have had them before, keep having them! Our time growing in the Glory and in His Word is priceless!

When I look at my yellow walls, I am reminded of His precious promises. That is the place where I gain strength to not quit, and not give up. I also rehearse the goodness of God in that place. I read aloud prophetic words that have been given to me and my family. I speak out the scriptures that declare He is for us, and not against us. I gain courage to continue to fight for my region and nation. Holy Spirit will often highlight a verse of scripture, remind me of a personal prophecy, or speak a fresh word for that moment. When I meditate and look at those yellow walls, I dream with God. I dream of the destiny that He has for my life, and my family's, for my church, my city, my region, my nation and the nations of the world.

> **"Everything that goes into a life of pleasing God has been miraculously given to us by getting to know, personally and intimately, the One who invited us to God. The best invitation we ever received! We were also given absolutely terrific promises to pass on to you – your tickets to participation in the life of God after you turned your back on a world corrupted by lust."**
> **– 2 Peter 1:3-4 MSG**

## *Butterflies and Fives...The Language of the Spirit*

As I have continued to stay the course, I have become much more aware of the supernatural ways of our Father and His Kingdom. His goodness and faithfulness have been on display in many ways, both large and small. It is our opportunity to know Him in this very intimate, personal and loving way.

He speaks in so many ways, some of which are signs that, at the very least make you wonder, and at best communicate with you in a very personal way. I have personally experienced gold dust appearing on me, and also others around me. I have felt the breeze, or wind, of the Spirit in times of worship. I have seen an angel once, and other times been very aware of their presence. I have been in meetings where people's teeth were filled with gold. It is our opportunity to keep our spirit in tune with Holy Spirit, and experience the real, fun and intimate ways He speaks to us.

Butterflies and fives started to manifest to me in 2014. Although I had been learning God's ways in this prophetic area for years, I was about to experience some very real and tangible acts of His love, and heightening of His voice. I had been gaining a greater awareness of butterflies in the past year. I already had many pretty decorations in my home with butterflies on them, and had always had an affection for them. Friends and family would give me cards, notepads and journals with butterflies on them. Then one day, I saw a beautiful, yellow butterfly as I was walking in my neighborhood. It was a summer day after a difficult season in my life.

Our church was experiencing spiritual, and natural, growth following a difficult year. We were making progress in the Kingdom, but the devil still comes to steal, kill and destroy. The difficult season in our church was followed by a difficult season in my personal life. Sometimes God allows shaking in our lives, in order for us to go deeper in Him, and gain more freedom in our relationship with Him, and with others.

At any rate, during that time I began to see butterflies when I would go for my walks. I had walked in our neighborhood every week for the six years we had lived there, and never seen butterflies. I would also see them in different random places, not just walking by some flowers that attracted them. I would notice how beautiful they were, and thank God for their beauty, and the feeling I got when I saw them. It's like He was loving on me, and encouraging me in a very personal way, reminding me of His faithfulness, His love, and His promise of restoration. Butterflies represent new life, transformation and new birth.

> *"It seemed no matter how much I would charge my devices during this season, they would still find their way back to 55%. At the very least I would get a good laugh, and ALL of the time thank God for His constant reminder of His grace, goodness and favor in my life, which is what the number 5 represents."*

Then I began to see butterflies daily, and not just on my walks.

The butterflies would fly right across my head or face on walks or in parking lots. I would see them outside my kitchen window, through the window at a business, or across my windshield as I was driving. Two days in a row, I saw double butterflies come across my windshield while driving on the highway. One day, I saw six butterflies! That's when I said, "Alright, God, I get it...you love me BIG! You are for me! You are with me! You will never leave me, and we are coming through this trial!" This realization was accompanied by tears and a beautiful, intimate time of worship. He was reminding me not to give up, but rather, to stay the course.

As I was seeing butterflies, my husband and I both started seeing numbers in series. God speaks prophetically to His children through numbers. Numbers have meanings, and often coincide with a scripture that Holy Spirit is speaking to us. My husband woke up one morning at 4:44 a.m. and on this same morning, I woke up at the same time. This was more of a miracle for me, since I am a pretty heavy sleeper, and not a morning person. I actually heard a crash, as if something fell off the wall. I guess the Lord knew I needed that for a wake-up call.

God spoke several scriptures to us as well as other Hebrew meanings of the number four. Steven continued waking up at 4:44 a.m., getting up to pray. One morning he woke up at 4:55 a.m., and that's when my season of butterflies turned into fives. I began to see the clock at 5:55. Throughout my day, I would look at a clock or open my phone and it would either be 1:55, 2:55, or 5:55 and my phone or iPad would constantly be at fifty-five percent charge. It seemed no matter how much I would charge my devices during this season, they would still find their way back to fifty-five percent!

At the very least I would get a good laugh, and ALL of the time thank God for His constant reminder of His grace, goodness and favor in my life, which is what the number five represents. I also began to thank God for the double fives: His double portion coming to us and to His people. That season transitioned us into the Hebraic year, 5775 and into 2015. I saw the number five so much, that I began to grow in my belief in His goodness, and His incredible ways that He speaks to us.

Seeing the number five continues to happen to this day. During the writing of this book, I have been overwhelmed, and encouraged, by seeing the number five over and over! I have seen double and triple fives in just about any way I could imagine seeing a series of numbers in my daily life. That said, it would be nice to say that we never have challenging days, or seasons of discouragement. Although we are learning not to partner with hopelessness or discouragement, it creeps in sometimes. We just don't let it stay. Learning His language can equip us to stay the course and not give up.

# Chapter 9
## Grace to Stay

In late August, 2016, my husband and I took our son to college in Nashville. I cried all of the way home to Texas! But before that, I had lovingly and playfully told my son, Christian, that I was going to deal with him being away from home for the first time by writing a book.

God had given me a timeline, and grace to take the next month off, in order to write as much as possible. I had a goal to finish the rough draft before I left for a ministry trip to Washington D.C. But wait! My plan didn't go so well. I finished everything but one chapter.

I had never experienced writer's block, so I wasn't sure if that was my problem, or what was, exactly.

I was just stuck. The title I had for this chapter didn't sound right anymore. I would block out my time, as I had previously done to write the other chapters, but to no avail. I would sit there, and have nothing, or I would get crazy interuptions.

> *"Thankfully, I didn't let those fruitless emotions set in. I stepped back and thought about what I have learned and experienced in life when things did not go as planned and I took the opportunity to rehearse the stuff I use."*

What about my plan and my timeline? Oh no! Panic tried to set in. What if I had gotten this far, with supernatural grace to write this book, but got stuck on one chapter, holding up my God-breathed plan for this book, launch date and all? Immediately, my confidence level started to drop. I was starting to get rattled over, in 'Texas -language', one stinking chapter!

Doubt and unbelief started to not just creep in, but roll in with a vengeance. I knew this was not fruitful, but just as in the movie "A Bug's Life," I couldn't look away, and it was going to kill me. Well, not really, but you know that's how we feel sometimes. Life is over! There's no hope!

Thankfully, I didn't let those fruitless emotions set in. I stepped back and thought about what I have learned and experienced in life when things did not go as planned. I took the opportunity to rehearse "the stuff I use". What is that, you ask? Well, this term I call, "the stuff I use", actually came with my iPhone.

One day, I was looking at my apps on my fairly new phone, and discovered a section that said,"stuff I use." I was puzzled because I didn't even know it was there. How could this be "stuff I use" when I don't use it? It turns out that this app came with the phone. It was filled with a compass, a calculator, a phone finder and many other helpful things. Well, now that I had found it, I would use it!

How many of us have access to a great, abundant source or supply of "stuff I use", such as principles of the Word of God and from the Spirit of God teaching us, and yet we either don't know these resources are there, or have never learned how to access them? In living to stay our course, we must use every tool available to us.

> *"Our Father keeps His promises to us. We are the Levites ministering to the Lord. How do we do that? We worship. We love. We trust. We are his chosen people and He will not abandon us. We have the blueprint of His Word and the help of Holy Spirit to enable us to stay the course."*

I began to rehearse the tools, or the "stuff I use", when fear, doubt, discouragement and the rest of the list comes my way. First, I knew I had to take a step back, and get into rest. I chose to rest in God's presence. We like to call this soaking worship. When I soak, or rest in His presence, I completely immerse myself in His unfailing love, and overwhelming protection. I quiet my emotions and feelings, and stay in the shadow of His wings. Not only did I rest spiritually, but I also rested physically. I chose not to enter into the panic, or fear, that can so easily beset us.

Many people quit, or give up on their destiny or assignment, when their plans get altered or changed. However, I have seen that there is something down on the inside of us, something innate, that does not want to quit, or give up. We see it in champion athletes, Olympic competitors and even on the playground at our schools. We want to win! We were made to succeed, and to conquer in life!

However, there is an endurance and perseverance required to win. The enemy has come to steal that "grace to stay" from our culture, but God has a keeping anointing available for us in this hour. The following is a "go to", but not exhaustive, list of "stuff I use" in my journey of staying the course:

*Stuff I Use:*
1. **God keeps His promises!**

> **"This is what the LORD says: If you can break my covenant with the day and the night so that one does not follow the other, only then will my covenant with my servant David be broken. Only then will he no longer have a descendant to reign on his throne. The same is true for my covenant with the Levitical priests who minister before me. And as the stars of the sky cannot be counted and the sand on the seashore cannot be measured, so I will multiply the descendants of my servant**

> **David and the Levites who minister before me...Have you noticed what people are saying?—'The LORD chose Judah and Israel and then abandoned them!' They are sneering and saying that Israel is not worthy to be counted as a nation. But this is what the LORD says: I would no more reject my people than I would change my laws that govern night and day, earth and sky. I will never abandon the descendants of Jacob or David, my servant, or change the plan that David's descendants will rule the descendants of Abraham, Isaac, and Jacob. Instead, I will restore them to their land and have mercy on them."**
>
> **- Jeremiah 33:20-22, 24-26 NLT**

Wow! Those are strong words of covenant. Our Father keeps His promises to us. We are the Levites ministering to the Lord. How do we do that? We worship. We love. We trust. We are his chosen peo-ple, and He will not abandon us. We have the blueprint of His Word, and the help of Holy Spirit to enable us to stay the course.

There have been times in my life that I questioned where God was in the midst of dark circumstances. I struggled to remember the covenant I had with Him. I wondered why things were happening the way they were. I didn't feel His great love, comfort and safety during the storms of life. However, He has always shown Himself faithful in the end. Remembering His promises in dark seasons will steadily lead us back into the light, and into life again. There are times when we feel the wind is knocked out of us, but He will restore us back to Himself.

## 2. Extravagant Worship and Crazy Praise

Extravagant worship has become my default and I absolutely love it! I have realized I am created for this, and guess what? So are you. God made us this way. He loves our worship and all-out devotion to Him. We are called to practice His presence. It can be our way of life. I am musical, so I always have a song in my head. I can't tell you how many times God speaks to me, and loves on me, through waking me up with a certain song, just for me, just for that day. I love the "song of the Lord" that can rise up in us in our darkest times, that can connect us to the light, and bring us to victory. Our worship is an ongoing love song to Jesus and it reverberates back from Him to us.

I have to say that there is something special that happens in our crazy praise. I'm talking loud, go for it, shouting, jumping, all-into-it praise! The kind of praise that shifts us into another gear in the Spirit. This kind of praise releases breakthrough. It usually happens when we make a decision to go higher, and deeper, in our worship to the Lord. I cannot tell you how many times I have experienced freedom

> *"Holiness is the standard of the day that attracts God's presence and favor in our lives. Living in purity and in holiness keeps us close to Him."*

in my life as a result of this kind of praise. I have observed this kind of corporate spiritual breakthrough most often when there has been heaviness, lack, or discouragement; or resulting from the influence of political or religious structures in a group, city, region or nation. I have experienced feelings of hopelessness, and wanting to give up, but I say, "God, you are bigger than all of this, so I'm just going to go for it in my praise, and I'm not going to let my emotions rule! I'm not going to hold anything back from You." This is the time that the Captain of the Host, Jesus, the Lion of Judah, comes in on the scene and the entire atmosphere changes. Joy, hope and so much more are released and restored.

> **"Let true lovers break out in praise, sing out from wherever they're sitting, Shout the high praises of God, brandish their swords in the wild sword-dance." - Psalms 149:5-6 MSG**

Many times my worship to God has been in faith. As a result, unwavering faith comes in, and puts me on a steady course. His wonderful presence removes doubt, creates hope and expectancy, and puts courage back into me. Our worship creates great intimacy with our Heavenly Father. Faith and direction are birthed out of that intimacy, along with an undeniable knowing that He is our Father, and that He is taking over our entire lives. This praise drowns out all lies from the enemy.

> "You take over. I'm about to die, my life an offering on God's altar. This is the only race worth running. I've run hard right to the finish, believed all the way. All that's left now is the shouting—God's applause! Depend on it, he's an honest judge. He'll do right not only by me, but by everyone eager for his coming."
>
> - 2 Timothy 4:6-8 MSG

## 3. Holiness: It's Not a "Back in the Day" Movement

I have shared this with my sons many times as they were growing up but it's important to keep our "streams clean." Living a holy, pure, clean life is our response to His incredible grace and love for us.

Since we live from the position of relationship and not rules, we choose to live consecrated and pure before Him because we want to, not because we have to. Holiness is the standard of the day that attracts God's presence, and favor, in our lives. Living in purity, and in holiness, keeps us close to Him. It's what makes us different, attractive, and unique in God. It's a safe and confident way to live. It's the Bible way and it's beautiful!

> "You're blessed when you stay on course, walking steadily on the road revealed by GOD.

You're blessed when you follow his directions, doing your best to find him. That's right—you don't go off on your own; you walk straight along the road he set. You, GOD, prescribed the right way to live; now you expect us to live it. Oh, that my steps might be steady, keeping to the course you set; Then I'd never have any regrets in comparing my life with your counsel. I thank you for speaking straight from your heart; I learn the pattern of your righteous ways. I'm going to do what you tell me to do; don't ever walk off and leave me." - Psalm 119:1-8 MSG

4. **Prayer and Fasting**

There are hundreds of books on prayer and fasting. I say, just do it. Live a fasted life. Pray every way possible. Allow Holy Spirit to pray through you. Be okay with tears, laughter, shouting and quiet. Stay yielded and hungry. Beni Johnson said, in her book *The Happy Intercessor*, "I don't choose travail; travail chooses me." What a true statement for prayer and fasting in general! There are so many ways to pray, commune, and talk with God. Just do it.

"Rejoice always! Pray constantly. Give thanks in everything, for this is God's will for you in Christ Jesus. Don't stifle the Spirit."

- 1 Thessalonians 5:16-19 HCSB

5. Unwavering Faith

"Do you see what this means—all these pioneers who blazed the way, all these veterans cheering us on? It means we'd better get on with it. Strip down, start running—and never quit! No extra spiritual fat, no parasitic sins. Keep your eyes on Jesus, who both began and finished this race we're in. Study how he did it. Because he never lost sight of where he was headed—that exhilarating finish in and with God—he could put up with anything along the way: Cross, shame, whatever. And now he's there, in the place of honor, right alongside God. When you find yourselves flagging in your faith, go over that story again, item by item, that long litany of hostility he plowed through. That will shoot adrenaline into your souls!"

- Hebrews 12:1-3 MSG

Jesus is our example. He always has been, and always will be. God placed Jesus on this earth so that we could live as He lived. The dictionary meaning of "stay the course" is to keep going strong to the end of a race or contest. The English dictionary says, "To continue doing something until it is finished, or until you achieve something you have planned to do." Jesus stayed the ultimate course for you and me when He said on the cross, "It is finished!"

> *"Jesus stayed the ultimate course for you and I when He said on the cross, 'It is finished!'"*

> "When Jesus had tasted it, he said, "It is finished!" Then he bowed his head and released his spirit." - John 19:30 NLT

## 6. Shameless Persistence

> "Then, teaching them more about prayer, he used this story: "Suppose you went to a friend's house at midnight, wanting to borrow three loaves of bread. You say to him, 'A friend of mine has just arrived for a visit, and I have nothing for him to eat.' And suppose he calls out from his bedroom, 'Don't bother me. The door is locked for the night, and my family and I are all in bed. I can't help you.' But I tell you this—though he

**won't do it for friendship's sake, if you keep knocking long enough, he will get up and give you whatever you need because of your shameless persistence. "And so I tell you, keep on asking, and you will receive what you ask for. Keep on seeking, and you will find. Keep on knocking, and the door will be opened to you. For everyone who asks, receives. Everyone who seeks, finds. And to everyone who knocks, the door will be opened." - Luke 11:5-10 NLT**

There is a 'breakthrough grace' that has been released in the spirit for this season and it is filled with "shameless persistence." There is an anointing released in this hour for us that says, "I know there's breakthrough there. I can't stop knocking because the next knock might be the knock that opens the door." There is a world of supernatural miracles available to us if we keep knocking, keep asking and keep seeking.

For example, I love that my husband is a persistent person. If you want a project completed and done correctly, he's your guy. He loves cars, and for a fun season in our lives, we had classic cars. He would buy them, fix them up, have fun driving them for a while and then sell them. Time and again, he would take those cars in to have something fixed, and the guys at the body shop would tell him that it couldn't be done. Wrong words for that guy! He would go home, get on the Internet, search out the problem, and go back to the body shop with the solution. Many times the car would get fixed, but there were always a few little things not fixed on them. He would go back and forth to the body shop, over and over again, until it was right.

Our boys were young at the time, and we would have to follow him to the body shop so he could drop the car off to get fixed, and pick him up from the body shop. The boys, and myself, to be honest, would sometimes get tired of the whole, "take the car to the body shop routine," but because of his shameless persistence, he came out with some sweet little rides. He developed a great relationship with the body shop guys, and clients liked to buy his cars because they knew they would be built right. Like Steven, we must continue to persist in our faith, until we have the answer we seek.

## *Stay the Course for Transformation*

Thankfully, after rehearsing the "stuff I use," I rested in my promises from the Lord. I knew the completion of this chapter would come. I knew that, as I put my trust in the Lord, it would be better than I could expect. My husband and I went on our ministry trip to D.C. While there, we walked the land in faith, and prayer, for revival and awakening. Thankfully, and not surprisingly, as we were leaving D.C. and taking off in the plane for Texas, the Lord began to give me the words to this chapter.

The day was cloudy, but as we took off and began to rise above the clouds, the sun was shining bright. There was a clarity returning to me, and a hope being restored for myself, and for our nation. That takeoff, and ascension into the clouds, was a wonderful prophetic picture of the Lord's promise and blueprint for our lives.

There is an unwavering faith, a relentless spirit, and a shameless persistence available from the spirit of God that has been released to the people of God. With it comes the grace to stay. There is grace to not give up! It's quite obvious that we are at a turning point in our nation, culture and time in history. Many have given up, and are just waiting for heaven, and to escape this world. For these people, it is difficult to see anything positive, and the lens through which they see life gets darker and darker as the days go on. They are a magnet for the negative.

> *"There is an unwavering faith, a relentless spirit and a shameless persistence available from the spirit of God that has been released to the people of God. With it comes the grace to stay."*

Yet, history tells us that when change and reformation takes place, there will always be that "remnant," that group of people or even one individual who will believe and fight and even give their lives for revival, transformation and reformation. At some point, they dig deep within themselves, connect with a belief system bigger than their own, and lock into that, knowing that they were born for such a time as this. They decide to not give up, not quit and to stay the course. I believe God is raising up an army of people for this time in history that will know who they are in Christ, take God at His Word, knowing that they were born for this, and run with their destiny!

**"I am not afraid. I was born to do this."**
**– Joan of Arc**

# Chapter 10
# From Declaration to Demonstration

Our words are so important. We have learned now, through avenues such as science and parenting, that our words matter. I could not write about being faithful to stay the course without talking about words. I think we can all say in life that we can see the power of our words, the good, bad and the ugly. I even think the church as a whole has a grasp on the power of our words and our declarations. We have grown in that knowledge in the last 50 years through great teaching. A word of encouragement to us in this season is to not shrink back, but declare with great authority, the word of the Lord over our lives, organizations, regions and nations.

> **"In the beginning God created the heavens and the earth. The earth was formless and empty, and darkness covered the deep waters. And the Spirit**

**of God was hovering over the surface of the waters. Then God said, 'Let there be light,' and there was light. - Genesis 1:3 NLT**

God created the earth when it was formless and empty. We, too, have the power to create by our declaration. At times, my husband and I may have a desire for a new ministry, or plan, and we talk about it a lot. We build it in our minds, and with our words. My husband Steven is a builder by nature! He loves starting and creating new things, so we spend hours talking those plans out. We talk about it so much, that we can see it clearly, before it is ever built.

Often, as we talked about a new project or plan, life would come into it. We would get more and more ideas as we declared our plan. Creativity would increase. God's presence and favor would light on it, and it would start to come forth in the natural. God has called everyone of us to dream, and be creative. God wants to bring His light to our desires and callings. He wants to invade our darkness with His light. In this present move of God, the spirit of God is moving to create, declare and birth us into our destinies.

> *"I even think the church as a whole has a grasp on the power of our words and our declaration. We have grown in that knowledge in the last 50 years through great teaching. A word of encouragement to us in this season is to not shrink back but declare with great authority the word of the Lord over our lives, organizations, regions and nations."*

> "The earth was without form and an empty waste, and darkness was upon the face of the very great deep. The Spirit of God was moving (hovering, brooding) over the face of the waters."
> - Genesis 1:2 AMP

*Declaration*

There is power and authority in what we speak. Following are some scriptures that show the power of our words, and others that are great declarations which we can make over our lives:

> "Death and life are in the power of the tongue, and they who indulge in it shall eat the fruit of it [for death or life]." - Proverbs 18:21 AMP
> "You are snared by the words of your mouth; You are taken by the words of your mouth."
> - Proverbs 6:2 NKJV

> "And they have defeated him by the blood of the Lamb and by their testimony. And they did not love their lives so much that they were afraid to die." - Revelation 12:11 NLT

> "Then I fell at his feet to worship him, but he said to me, "Don't do that! I am a fellow slave

with you and your brothers who have the testimony about Jesus. Worship God, because the testimony about Jesus is the spirit of prophecy."

- Revelation 19:10 HCSB

"I will extol You, my God, O King; And I will bless Your name forever and ever. Every day I will bless You, And I will praise Your name forever and ever...One generation shall praise Your works to another, And shall declare Your mighty acts....Men shall speak of the might of Your awesome acts, And I will declare Your greatness...All Your works shall praise You, O LORD, And Your saints shall bless You. They shall speak of the glory of Your kingdom, And talk of Your power."

- Psalms 145:1, 2, 4, 6, 10, 11 NKJV

"With their words, the godless destroy their friends, but knowledge will rescue the righteous." - Proverbs 11:9 NLT

"Upright citizens are good for a city and make it prosper, but the talk of the wicked tears it apart."

- Proverbs 11:11 NLT

> **"The generous will prosper; those who refresh others will themselves be refreshed."**
> **- Proverbs 11:25 NLT**

We will SEE the change that God wants us to walk in, as we speak it out. Our declaration is key as we stay the course. You might want to check your words, and go on a "negativity fast" from time to time. We've done it and it works! Our worship is one of the best ways we declare His goodness in our lives. As we worship and pray, His spirit leads our minds, and we therefore speak the words that He wants us to declare over our life.

**Declare Over Your Life and Family:**

1. Divine Access:

    > **"And that's not all. You will have complete and free access to God's kingdom, keys to open any and every door: no more barriers between heaven and earth, earth and heaven. A yes on earth is yes in heaven. A no on earth is no in heaven."**
    > **- Matthew 16:19 MSG**

    > **"I will give you the keys of the kingdom of heaven; and whatever you bind (declare to be improper and unlawful) on earth must be what is already bound in heaven; and whatever you loose**

(declare lawful) on earth must be what is already loosed in heaven." - Matthew 16:19 AMP

"I will give him the key to the house of David—the highest position in the royal court. When he opens doors, no one will be able to close them; when he closes doors, no one will be able to open them." - Isaiah 22:22 NLT

2. Favor and Authority:

"For You, Lord, bless the righteous one; You surround him with favor like a shield."

- Psalms 5:12 HCSB

"You also will command nations you do not know, and peoples unknown to you will come running to obey, because I, the LORD your God, the Holy One of Israel, have made you glorious."

- Isaiah 55:5 NLT

3. Transformation:

"Don't copy the behavior and customs of this world, but let God transform you into a new person by changing the way you think. Then you will learn to know God's will for you, which is good and pleasing and perfect."

- Romans 12:2 NLT

## *Demonstration*

Declarations are not just for the sake of making declarations. They are intended to activate faith in our hearts that we will have what we are declaring. This declaration brings about a demonstration which leads to transformation in our lives, businesses, churches, regions and nations. When we experience transformation, we will see reformation.

**Transformation:**

a thorough or dramatic change in form or appearance.

**Reformation:**

1) the action or process of reforming an institution or practice; 2) a 16th-century movement for the reform of abuses in the Roman Catholic Church ending in the establishment of the Reformed and Protestant Churches.

I find it interesting that the last reformation is listed within the definition of the name. God is preparing us now for a new Reformation. The year 2017 marks 500 years from the beginning of the Protestant Reformation. This new reformation will happen as we partner with Holy Spirit, first in our own life, and then we will see the ripple effect. We are truly being prepared to go from declaration to demonstration!

> *"This new reformation will happen as we partner with Holy Spirit, first in our own life and then we will see the ripple effect. We are truly being prepared to go from declaration to demonstration!"*

## *A Season of Accomplishment*

As we walk in a life of declaring God's word, we can surely expect to see accomplishment. This is the way of the Kingdom. At the beginning of 2016, the Lord spoke to us that this would be, "A Year of Accomplishment," for both our lives and our church. We have watched God supernaturally carry this out. We saw accomplishments of debt cancellation, buildings built and completed, a book written, new ministries formed and established, projects started and completed, new business endeavors started and carried out, and the list goes on. God is faithful to His Word.

> **"After greeting them, Paul gave a detailed account of the things God had accomplished among the Gentiles through his ministry."**
> **- Acts 21:19 NLT**

As we read this scripture, we learn that God was working through Paul to bring about the accomplishments. God wants to work through you and me. It is His plan to reach the world, and fulfill His destiny upon our lives. We should expect to see great accomplishments in this present move of God. There will be dreams and desires that you have held in your heart for a very long time that God will fulfill in this season. We must stay our course so that we can see the accomplishment when it comes. Expect to see answered prayers, suddenlies, awakening, revival, great joy, freedom and miracles! God is raising up men and women who treasure the Word of God in a fresh, new way. We will not be living on theory, or the way things have always been done; rather, we will feast upon living revelation from the Word of God.

> *"In this present move of God, we should expect to see great accomplishments. Expect to see answered prayers, suddenlies, awakening, revival, great joy, freedom and miracles!"*

As we saturate our lives with God's Word, it will accomplish much fruit in our lives.

> **"The rain and snow come down from the heavens and stay on the ground to water the earth. They cause the grain to grow, producing seed for the farmer and bread for the hungry. It is the same with my word. I send it out, and it always produces fruit. It will accomplish all I want it to, and it will prosper everywhere I send it. You will live in joy and peace. The mountains and hills will burst into song, and the trees of the field will clap their hands!" - Isaiah 55:10-12 NLT**

In the world, there are many unknowns, and seemingly minute-by-minute changes. Every day we see disturbing and alarming news. How will we LIVE in joy and peace? God's Word and His presence will be our meat and our wine. In his book, *Hosting the Presence: Unveiling Heaven's Agenda*, Bill Johnson said, "When God is serving wine, drink. When He's serving bread, eat."

I have determined to live my life to the end, doing just that. When we make His Word and His presence the main thing in our life, we can expect to see accomplishments. Remember, He is able. Jesus beats the odds. He is a miracle maker!

**"Now all glory to God, who is able, through his mighty power at work within us, to accomplish infinitely more than we might ask or think."**
**- Ephesians 3:20 NLT**

A strong key to staying the course is learning to praise God for the accomplishments before they happen. You will, "praise yourself happy," as the saying goes. Our blueprint for this season will be companies of people that praise, and brag about, the goodness of God. He is worthy! Our ministry is honored to be connected with ministries such as David's Tent in Washington, D.C., that are lifting up worship and praise, nonstop, twenty-four hours a day, seven days a week to God - simply because He is worthy of a nation's praise. We have taken teams to lead worship there every year since its beginning in 2012. There's nothing like leading worship in that tent in the heart of our nation's capital, knowing that we are praising God in advance for what only He can do in our nation. As we worship, we call forth God's redemptive plans for the United States of America.

> *"God is calling His sons and daughters to arise, awaken and answer the call to greatness and accomplishment, not just for ourselves but for the world around us."*

> "Yahweh, You are my God; I will exalt You. I will praise Your name, for You have accomplished wonders, plans formed long ago, with perfect faithfulness." - Isaiah 25:1 HCSB

*Are Your Ears Awake? Listen to the Wind Words!*

We have been and are still in a time of shifting, preparing, rearranging, and making the Bride ready for what is to happen in this day. God has such an amazing blueprint from His Word, and He is blowing with His spirit on each step that we should take. God is raising up love-sick warriors who will serve at His good pleasure. We will be laid-down lovers of God, who have given all for the One who is All! We will rise up as a strong army, to carry out His plans and purposes on this earth. Jesus truly is the desire of the nations! God is calling His sons and daughters to arise, awaken and answer the call to greatness and accomplishment, not only for ourselves but for the world around us.

> "Here's the reward I have for every conqueror, everyone who keeps at it, refusing to give up: You'll rule the nations, your Shepherd-King rule as firm as an iron staff, their resistance fragile as clay pots. This was the gift my Father gave me; I pass it along to you—and with it, the Morning Star! "Are your ears awake? Listen. Listen to the

**Wind Words, the Spirit blowing through the churches." - Revelation 2:26-29 MSG**

## *That Day*

We are going to a new place, standing in a new grace.
With confidence we say this is that day.
Winds are blowing with a new force;
River's flowing from a new source.
With confidence we say this is that day.

This is the day that You have made and we rejoice!
It's the appointed time that we've been waiting for.
This is that day, harvest is here! It's a due season.
This is the day You have made. This is that day!

Fall on us Your sons and daughters, fill us Holy Spirit now.
With confidence we say this is that day.
Make us healthy, make us holy, ready for the road ahead.
With confidence we say this is that day.

Words & Music by Steven Charles
© Cross the World Music

## Chapter 11
## Experience His Presence, See His Glory

"In the last days, the mountain of the LORD's house will be the highest of all - the most important place on earth. It will be raised above the other hills, and people from all over the world will stream there to worship. People from many nations will come and say, "Come, let us go up to the mountain of the LORD, to the house of Jacob's God. There he will teach us his ways, and we will walk in his paths." For the LORD's teaching will go out from Zion; his word will go out from Jerusalem." - Isaiah 2:2-3 NLT

That day is this day! Oh, how many have dreamed of this time, and prayed and prophesied into it. My heart is full of gratitude for those who have stayed their course through the years of history on this earth. I am so thankful they did not quit when it got tough. They carried the torch throughout history.

My husband's family was in the Moravian church. How grateful I am for their steadfast commitment to a twenty four hours a day, seven days a week, nonstop prayer meeting that lasted one hundred years. I have been to the village in Herrnhut, Germany, whose prayers birthed a great revival, a world-wide missions movement, and influenced the ministry of John Wesley. John Wesley and his associates would go on to lead the Great Awakening that brought many people in England and America into the Kingdom of God.

I am grateful for the men and women of the Azusa revival, which birthed the Pentecostal movement in which I, and many others, was raised. I am grateful for my parents, and many family members, who have stayed the course for revival and glory outpouring in my lifetime. I grew up hearing stories of my mom fasting, and praying for hours over my dad while he was traveling in ministry. As a result of their faithfulness, many were saved and transformed by the Holy Spirit as my father preached the gospel. The "Acts of the Apostles" are still being written! I could fill pages and pages of the histories of Christian men and women – apostles, warriors, presidents and world leaders – who have stayed their course, and in doing so, changed history.

You and I are called for such a time as this to change history, too! As we experience His presence and see His glory, we will carry His presence and display His glory for all to see. I want to share an open vision I had in 2014, after a wonderful time of worship and prayer one day with the Lord. I saw so much, and it was so clear, and real to me. It was like watching a movie. I can't wait for the real thing! Be encouraged in this season. We have been going through a narrow place of transition, to prepare for the enlargement that God is bringing us into.

Here is what I saw:

"I saw an army of worshippers, glory lovers, loving their life not unto death. They were walking among the dead, dark places on this earth. Everything the water of the spirit touched through them lived. Everything came alive. The darkness turned to bright, vibrant, light. It was like no other anointing I have ever seen. A thick cloud of glory appeared.

I saw a glimpse into the revival realm that is coming. Children, teenagers, and adults of all ages were being swept up into this amazing cloud of glory. They were filled with blue and red light. There were bolts of electricity going out. That was the fire of the Holy Spirit, instantly awakening and bringing people to life."

One encounter with His Glory, and everything changes. Stay for the Glory. We can receive the anointing of Holy Spirit, and the mantles from others that have gone before us. It's coming! Much of it is already beginning.

In May of 2016, I had a Heavenly encounter where I was in a green room, or a holding room. Many of us were preparing and waiting to go out into a large arena. In this green room, God's presence was so strong. Holy Spirit was swirling all around us. It was like a sauna. It was a thick glory. There were Angels of Provision, Glory, Revival and Rest assigned to each one of us.

**"Even the wilderness and desert will be glad in those days. The wasteland will rejoice and blossom with spring crocuses. Yes, there will be an abundance of flowers and singing and joy! The deserts will become as green as the mountains of Lebanon, as lovely as Mount Carmel or the plain of Sharon. There the LORD will display his glory, the splendor of our God. With this news, strengthen those who have tired hands, and encourage those who have weak knees. Say to those with fearful hearts, 'Be strong, and do not fear, for your God is coming to destroy your enemies. He is coming to save you.' And when he comes, he will open the eyes of the blind and unplug the ears of the deaf. The lame will leap like a deer, and those who cannot speak**

**will sing for joy! Springs will gush forth in the wilderness, and streams will water the wasteland. The parched ground will become a pool, and springs of water will satisfy the thirsty land. Marsh grass and reeds and rushes will flourish where desert jackals once lived."**

**- Isaiah 35:1-7 NLT**

Our wonderful Father longs to display His glory to His sons and daughters. I believe He has saved the best for last. We are going to experience His presence and see His glory! He is the God of miracles.

One day I went into our house of prayer alone to pray, and just be with the Lord. I had been having a challenging week, and I felt like a pressure cooker getting ready to erupt. Knowing that was not good for me or anyone else around me, I decided to take some extra time with Him. The first two hours or so, I mainly just sat in God's presence. I needed Him to unpack all of the emotions I was feeling, and allow Holy Spirit to bring me into His order, and peace. I sat with the Lord and to be honest, I replied to a few texts and made a to-do list during that time. I didn't feel a blast of His glory or have the encounter of a lifetime – I just stayed with Him. I got in close to Him, under the "shadow of His wings" (Psalms 91).

Just as I was planning to leave, a particular song came on that

Holy Spirit had been reminding me of, and singing to me, in the midst of my chaos all week. At that moment, I linked in with the King of Glory, and He came in to meet me in only the way that He does. He displayed His Glory and gave me a divine alignment with Heaven. He strengthened my tired hands, encouraged my weak knees, and fear was replaced with peace and faith.

For the next hour, I met with the King of Glory! I came up to where He was, gained His divine perspective, and declared His purposes into the atmosphere. I left that place of prayer a different person than when I came in. Every conversation I had with others that day was filled with life, faith, joy and encouragement. He truly is the God of miracles, and He wants to display His glory over our lives. That day I came out of agreement with the doubt and unbelief that had been crowding my mind and spirit, and entered back into my agreement with Heaven's reality.

The glory is worth waiting for. It's worth staying for. Back in the day, the saints would tarry or wait until He came. He has prepared a spring of living water in the midst of our wilderness. I don't mind waiting, how about you?

### *Revival Glory!*

I have loved reading the Glory books written by the late revivalist and prophetess, Ruth Ward Heflin. I am honored to stay in the home that she stayed in while in Washington, D.C., when I go there for ministry. She loved our nation and loved having a home in our nation's capital. She also had a great call, and ministry, to Israel. Ruth lived in Jerusalem, as well, and she was used by the Lord as an ambassador of peace and healing to that land. She loved Israel with all of her heart! One of my favorite books of hers is *Revival Glory*. She wrote, "What God wants to do in these last days, can only be accomplished in the glory realm."

We are entering into things that can only happen in God's glory. His manifest presence is invading our lives in everything we do. Spending time in His glory is one of my very favorite things. It's always new, fresh, heavy, light, full of joy, tears flow easily and miracles happen all in one space of time. I wonder, how can I experience all of those emotions, all at once? He is good like that.

There is a spiritual alignment that takes place in the glory. Need an attitude adjustment? Get in the glory. Need healing in your mind, body or spirit? Get in the glory. Everything we have need of is available in His presence. Throughout the years, my testimony over and over again is that God's glory changes everything. I am still learning to stay the course in this area.

Many times we forfeit the bounty of God's presence, because we aren't willing to press through to the other side. We come to corporate worship meetings weighed down with life's challenges, and instead of pressing in to get strength, peace, freedom, and whatever else we need, we stop short. We give up, because we don't like the transition from the natural, into the spiritual world. Our flesh likes the depression, sadness, oppression, and the "plain ole funk" we get into. We give in to our flesh, instead of leaning into the One that can release freedom, healing and forgiveness.

As a child, I grew up in tent revivals. I was a part of all-night prayer meetings, and revival meetings that "stick with you" when go home. As an adult, I have experienced awesome times of worship in my home, in our house of prayer and church, and in gatherings with the Body of Christ. I love talking about, and experiencing, the glory.

I am hungry for that day! The Holy Spirit has been speaking to me, confirming through His prophets, that those days are coming in even greater measure. We must be ready, excited, and expectant of His revival glory to awaken His Bride, bring in the harvest, and pour out His Spirit in full force!

It's already happening, but what we see now is just a trickle. Conviction of sin, limbs growing out, and the priests (people) unable to stand, all in one meeting! Wow! This sounds like revival glory to me. It's coming like a locomotive. It will be unstoppable. This will be a demonstration of His great love for this nation, and the nations of the world.

I see revival glory happening in small towns, villages, high rise buildings, neighborhoods, business offices, in schools, on social media, on the news, in our churches, and in stadiums. He's coming! We have an opportunity to be a part of this grand story, this remarkable moment in history that will change everything.

> **"Staying with it—that's what God requires. Stay with it to the end. You won't be sorry, and you'll be saved. All during this time, the good news— the Message of the kingdom—will be preached all over the world, a witness staked out in every country. And then the end will come."**
> **- Matthew 24:11-14 MSG**

I wanted to share more of the context of the above scripture, in another version, just to remind us of the words of Jesus. The full counsel of God, and His word, will carry us in this movement. Jesus tells His disciples what is to come. He lays out the plan for them. I love that He tells them, "the one who endures to the end will be saved." Jesus encourages them in this entire chapter to stay their course.

> **"Jesus told them, "Don't let anyone mislead you, for many will come in my name, claiming, 'I am the Messiah.' They will deceive many. And you will hear of wars and threats of wars, but don't**

panic. Yes, these things must take place, but the end won't follow immediately. Nation will go to war against nation, and kingdom against kingdom. There will be famines and earthquakes in many parts of the world. But all this is only the first of the birth pains, with more to come. Then you will be arrested, persecuted, and killed. You will be hated all over the world because you are my followers. And many will turn away from me and betray and hate each other. And many false prophets will appear and will deceive many people. Sin will be rampant everywhere, and the love of many will grow cold. But the one who endures to the end will be saved. And the Good News about the Kingdom will be preached throughout the whole world, so that all nations will hear it; and then the end will come.

- Matthew 24:4-14 NLT

I am grateful for my spiritual heritage. My parents grew up in the Assemblies of God church. They began traveling in ministry when they were very young, and first got married. Until I started school, we traveled in tent revivals, and revivals in churches that would last for months at a time. I am a product of the Pentecostal church. The pastor in the church that I grew up in was saved, and discipled, under the ministry of William Branham. He lived, and was buried, in Indiana, in the town that I grew up in.

I am also a product of the Charismatic movement, the Brownsville revival, and Bethel Church in Redding, California, just to name a few. I have been influenced, and blessed, by many streams of the Body of Christ. I have had the five-fold ministry speak into my life. I've been ministered to at ladies' retreats, conferences, small groups, and home groups. I am a product of many wonderful men and women of God. I am a product of the Church.

Maybe you are reading this and that is not your story. Maybe you have never received Jesus as your Savior. You can get in the race today. Maybe the church has hurt you, and only labeled you as damaged goods. That's okay – God loves you and wants you back in the race. As we say in Texas, get back up on the horse, get in the saddle and ride. We have the opportunity to take up the mantle, carry the baton and finish our race. There is grace available for you and me, to stay our course.

> **"When the Lord restored the fortunes of Zion, we were like those who dream. Our mouths were filled with laughter then, and our tongues with shouts of joy. Then they said among the nations, "The Lord has done great things for them." The Lord had done great things for us; we were joyful.**

**Restore our fortunes, Lord, like watercourses in the Negev. Those who sow in tears will reap with shouts of joy. Though one goes along weeping, carrying the bag of seed, he will surely come back with shouts of joy, carrying his sheaves."**
**- Psalms 126:1-6 HCSB**

It's going to be worth it! All of the tears. All of the times you wanted to quit, and run away. All of the times you chose to stay, when everything in you wanted to leave, and say, "I'm done."

Harvest is here, my friend. Shouts of joy are your song. The Lord has done, and is doing, great things for you. Don't give up. Don't quit, my sons and daughters! Ride that horse, daughter of Zion. Hold that sword high, oh man of God. Fight the good fight, and run the race set before you! Stay your course!

**"Therefore, since we are surrounded by such a huge crowd of witnesses to the life of faith, let us strip off every weight that slows us down, especially the sin that so easily trips us up. And let us run with endurance the race God has set before us." - Hebrews 12:1 NLT**

## About the Author

Camilla has the spirit of a trailblazer, and is a catalyst in what God is doing, and wants to do, in this present move of God. She carries the presence of God, and is pressing in for revival for her region. She has a huge heart for the nations, and to see the Kingdom manifest.

Camilla speaks and sings regularly for conferences, churches and other Christian events. She has a passion for God's Word, and longs for real transformation for the body of Christ. Camilla believes that true revival is His arrival! Camilla encourages everyone to, "experience His presence and see His glory." She desires to see transformation for the East Texas area, in this nation, and into all the nations of the earth. Camilla encourages all believers to "Stay the Course", and walk in their God-given inheritance.

Camilla pastors Bethesda Church in Lindale, Texas, with her husband, Steven. Bethesda Church is an apostolic, revival hub for East Texas. Bethesda is the campus home for Bethesda Church School of Supernatural Ministry, East Texas House of Prayer, Transformation Center, and the Hub Coffee Shop. Camilla has recorded five music projects, including "Windows of Heaven", and "Personal Encounter." She travels nationally, and internationally, in ministry and prophetic prayer events.

She and Steven have two sons, Cameron and Christian, and make their home in Lindale, Texas.

CamillaCharles.com
bethesdachurchtx.com

## ABOUT THE ARTIST

Janet Hyun is one of the leading artists of the prophetic art movement and has an insatiable desire to see this generation impacted for the Kingdom of God. Her works are well recognized both in the United States and abroad and have been displayed worldwide in New York, Texas, Taiwan, Korea, and more. She has been featured in newspaper and magazine articles and interviews within the Christian community.

She is currently the director of Radiance International Gallery in Hollywood CA.

www.JanetHyun.com.

CAMILLA CHARLES

www.ingramcontent.com/pod-product-compliance
Lightning Source LLC
Chambersburg PA
CBHW051837090426
42736CB00011B/1856